TRAILS AWAY / *COLORADO*
Quick Escapes for Bikes, Blades, and Boots

also by Glen Hanket:

TAKE A BIKE
A Guide to the Denver Area's Urban Bike Trails

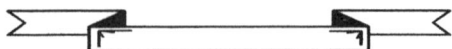

UNDERWEAR BY THE ROADSIDE
LitterWalk Coast-to-Coast

– the story of Glen and his wife Susan, who spent twelve months walking from Maine to Oregon, picking up four tons of trash and discovering the 'real' America.

See the back of this book for an excerpt from *Underwear by the Roadside.*

For information on ordering either of these books, see the order blank on the last page.

TRAILS AWAY / COLORADO

Quick Escapes for Bikes, Blades, & Boots

by Glen Hanket

CAK Publishing _____

PO Box 953   Broomfield, CO 80038

Published by CAK Publishing, PO Box 953, Broomfield CO 80038

Publisher's Catalog-in-Publication
                (Provided by Quality Books, Inc)

Hanket, Glen
    Trails away Colorado : quick escapes for bikes, blades, & boots /
by Glen Hanket. – 1st ed.
    p. cm.
    Includes index.
    ISBN: 0-9657833-2-4

    1. Trails–Colorado–Guidebooks. 2. Colorado–Guidebooks.
I. Title.

F774.3H36 1999   917.8804'33
                        QBI99-500287

dedicated to **A. William 'Bill' Padilla**

who accompanied me on many of these rides (and who
has no trouble in bicycling over Vail Pass)

TABLE OF CONTENTS

INTRODUCTION

Bicycles have been around for more than 200 years. In 1790 Frenchman Comte Mede de Sivrac invented a wooden scooter-like vehicle called a celerifere, used for propelling himself around the paths in formal gardens. This precursor to bicycles had two equal-sized wheels, but no steering mechanism!

In the 1800s, inventors improved the design considerably. By the end of the century bicycles were popular throughout the United States. Many people used them for recreation or commuting, and bike clubs flourished in major cities. Soon, though, the growing popularity of automobiles relegated bikes to the status of toys – something for kids, of course, but not a means of transportation.

In the 1960s, another innovation breathed new life in bicycles – gears! Three-speed, and later ten-speed, bikes became popular, sparking a renaissance in sales. Soon adults discovered that cycling, beside being fun, could help free them from the smog-and-traffic clogged streets of the city.

If they had a place to ride, that is. At that point, very few American locales had any designated off-street networks of paths for cyclists to use. However, a public with more and more leisure time began demanding more outlets for recreation. Governments responded by developing more parks and recreational paths, and by requiring developers to add open space and paths to any developments they fathered.

And the paths aren't just for bikes! Roller skates, an invention that predated the bicycle by sixty years, has also seen a surge in usage in the last decade. Credit for that can go to a 1980s innovation: in-line wheels. At first limited to hockey players, interest in the sport grew in 1986 with the introduction of a recreational in-line skate.

The explosive growth of trails recently is also the result of citizen activism. Groups of volunteers, united by their passion for trails, have provided the impetus for several of the major trail projects in the state. Often it requires long hours and endless patience to fight an uncaring bureaucracy, but the rewards in the end make it worthwhile.

I have listed in this book the main trails that I could find in my travels across the state. Every trail included is accessible to any bike, road ('skinny-tire') or mountain ('fat-tire'). No single- or double-track trails are covered here. In addition, most of the trails are paved or concrete, which makes them suitable for in-line skaters. The end-to-end distance on most trails ranges from five to eighteen miles. The few trails shorter than that were usually included because they form the beginning of a path that should grow in the next few years.

RULES OF THE ROAD

So you've reached the trailhead. Now you're ready to fly down the pavement, setting a new land speed record, right?

WRONG!

One of the biggest challenges facing trail users is retaining the right to use those trails. Not everyone welcomes trails in their area, and many people actively fight to have them removed from their property or neighborhoods. They cite out-of-control bicyclists injuring bystanders or hikers trashing public lands as ammunition in their fight against the paths. Unless we're all careful, a few thoughtless individuals could make us lose the wonderful paths throughout the state.

To prevent that, trail users have adopted the 'rules of the road'. The ten common-sense rules:

1. Cyclists and skaters should yield to horses and hikers.
2. Cyclists and skaters should maintain control at all times. This means keeping your speed within reasonable limits, and slowing down when approaching blind curves.
3. Obey all signs and postings.
4. Respect public property. Close any gates you opened, and don't damage someone's land.
5. Wear a helmet when cycling and pads when skating.
6. Do not obstruct a path by stopping in the middle of it.
7. Always walk or ride on the right.
8. When passing someone, call out to warn them.
9. Do not litter!
10. Use extra caution when wearing headphones. You may not hear someone warning you from behind.

Cycling or skating in Colorado presents additional challenges. There are several things to beware of to stay safe on the trails:

* Dehydration: During the hot summer months, you use a lot of fluids while exercising. Be sure to always carry enough water for your ride or hike, and then add a little more.

* Weather. Especially at high altitudes, the weather can change dramatically in a short time. You should keep spare clothing and coverings with you, in case those beautiful billowing clouds turn black when they get overhead.
* Sun. It takes years for skin cancer to develop, but more cases are discovered every year. Unless you think the leathery look is the way to go, use a sunscreen of 25 SPF or above. Also consider riding or skating before 10 o'clock or after 3, when the rays aren't as bad.
* Altitude. Unless you live in the high country, the elevation in the mountains may take quite a bit out of you. Even the fittest flatlander may find themselves short of breath while trying to conquer Vail Pass.
* Wildlife. Some of the trails may provide the opportunity to experience wildlife. Just remember – wildlife are wild and unpredictable. Beware of mountain lions and rattlesnakes, and treat all animals with respect.
* Spares. Always carry spares and a tool kit. You don't want to get stranded on an isolated stretch of trail at dusk!

HOW TO USE THIS BOOK

This book is divided into seven sections, with each section covering the trails in that area. All trails may be ridden with any type bicycle; no single- or double-track trails are included here. Most of the trails are also suitable for in-line skaters – check the 'Surface' description on the top of each writeup to insure that it is not a dirt or crushed gravel path. (However, some of the paved paths may be too weathered for a comfortable ride.) Of course, any of these trails are appropriate for a short walk.

Certain maps include symbols to describe landmarks you may pass. The symbols and meanings are:

city hall or offices		Visitor's Center	
gardens		parking / trailhead	
golf course		camping	
courthouse		hospital	
ball fields		tennis courts	
school		rodeo / fairgrounds	
swimming		ski area	
post office		playground	
marina		library	

WESTERN SLOPE

That portion of Colorado collectively termed the 'Western Slope' has an incredible diversity. The terrain ranges from high desert in the north, past the buttes and mesas in the Grand Valley, to the scenic San Juan mountains in the south. Much of the land is owned by federal agencies, and the area hosts six of the state's National Parks sites: Curecanti National Recreation Area; Colorado, Dinosaur, Hovenweep, and Black Canyon of the Gunnison National Monuments; and Mesa Verde National Park.

The area excels in opportunities for bicycling. Many of the towns have recognized the demand for recreation paths, planning and building trails for their populace. In addition, activist groups have lobbied for longer trails, tying together city parks, national forests, and BLM land into regional trails. Two of the longer trails proposed for the region: a 30-mile-plus trail along the Colorado River from Fruita to Palisade and beyond; and a 50-mile trail linking Telluride, Ridgway, and Ouray. Far-range plans include linking those two via Montrose and Delta.

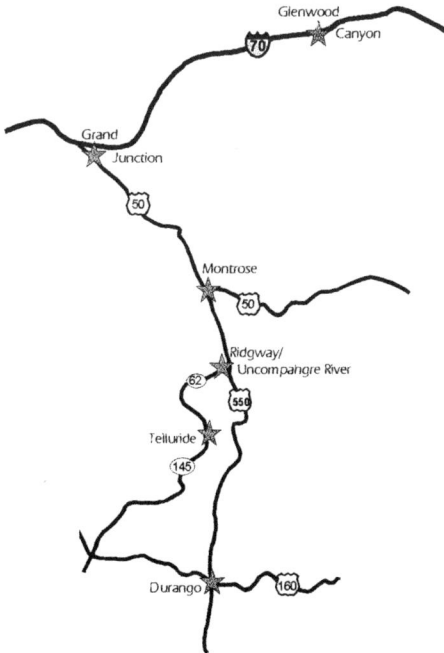

TRAIL: *Animas River / Durango*
DISTANCE: *3.8 (path) + 1.0 (street) miles*
SURFACE: *paved*
DIFFICULTY: *easy – some traffic on city streets*

As it did in most of the mountain towns in Colorado, mining played a major role in the history of Durango. Rather than being the site of gold strikes, it sprung forth as a rail hub for the ore traffic. Two National Historic Districts preserve the town's 19th-century feel. The restored Durango-Silverton Narrow Gauge Railroad attracts crowds for the 8-hour round trip through a remote canyon, exposing the rider to spectacular San Juan Mountains scenery.

Today Durango's fame as a mountain biking Mecca extends worldwide. Hundreds of miles of trails lace through the backcountry, and local riders bagged five gold and silver medals at the 1990 World Mountain Bike Championships. If you hope to come down and ride during the Labor Day weekend, be forewarned – other cyclists pack the town. An annual gathering of motorcyclists led by Senator Ben Nighthorse Campbell make hotel rooms a hard find. Many rooms are booked a year in advance.

'Skinny tire' bikers can snatch a few thrills here, also. Short trails in the north and south sections of the city can be linked by a quick ride through downtown. Both trails closely follow El Rio de las Animas Perdidas, 'the River of Lost Souls'.

In the north, the trail begins in the city park at 29th St & E 3rd Ave. To get there, take US550/Main Ave to 32nd St, head east to cross the river, and turn right on 3rd. The trail enters a wild stretch along the Animas River as it leaves the park. After crossing the river, it meets Junction Creek (0.7) in another city park. A side trail here runs upstream 0.2 miles to athletic fields. The main path continues beside the railroad tracks, finally crossing the river to end (1.2) in a pocket park on E 2nd Ave.

To connect to the southern stretch, you need to take a

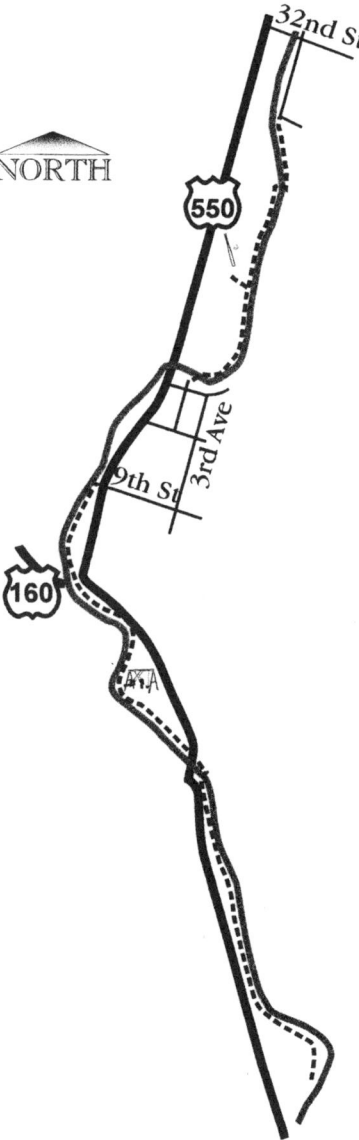

quick tour of the city. Head east (left) on 15th St one block, south (right) on 3rd for six blocks, and five blocks west (right) on 9th St. The trail begins again across the street, on the east back of the Animas. This 1.0 mile city tour is not strenuous, and the traffic is not heavy.

Head south on the paved trail behind hotels and businesses. After crossing under US160, the buildings disappear, exposing undeveloped hillsides. The trail follows the river around Gateway Park, where kayakers play in season. Bumpers hang from ropes strung across the river, defining courses to challenge the paddlers.

At mile 1.4 you pass under US160/US550, and soon cross the river. This land, south of Durango proper, has not been defiled by development. Old trees shade the trail, and traffic noises disappear under the roar of the river. Slowly the trail climbs a bluff to look down on the Animas, ending (2.6) in a dead end behind a stand of houses.

WHAT ELSE:

Durango is a fine base from which to explore the San Juan Mountains. This vacationland offers enough to warrant a short or long stay. Perhaps the town's most famous attraction is the Durango-Silverton Narrow Gauge Railroad, a forty-five mile rail trip through a narrow canyon unreachable by car. Allow for an eight-hour round trip when reserving tickets; each direction takes three hours and you'll want to wander around Silverton.

Further afield are Anasazi sites preserved under the National Park Service. Mesa Verde National Park, site of the world's largest cliff dwellings, lies an hour's drive west of Durango. Another hour further west, you can explore the isolated ruins enclosed by Hovenweep National Monument. These six sites feature, not cliff dwelling, but tall Anasazi stone towers.

As the largest town in the region, Durango has all the services you would expect. Hotels and restaurants abound, and bicycles can be rented in town. Camping is available outside of town.

TRAIL:	*San Miguel River / Telluride*
DISTANCE:	*3.3 miles*
SURFACE:	*smooth pavement*
DIFFICULTY:	*easy*

Gold and silver strikes brought throngs of people to the San Juan Mountains in the late nineteenth century. 1883 saw the platting of Columbia, a gold camp in a box canyon near the head of the San Miguel River. In the early 1890s, the town (renamed Telluride – a slurring of "to hell you ride!", some say) boasted 5,000 people, a railroad spur, and buildings ranging from grand Victorian mansions to gambling halls.

The town declined with the mining industry, nearly drying up before discovering a new life with 'white gold' – snow. The ski area officially opened in December 1972, and recreation dollars revitalized the town. Soon it became as popular in summer as in winter, with festivals (bluegrass, chamber music, hang gliding, wild mushroom, and the famous Film Festival), jeep rides, kayaking, hiking, and more.

Though it is far from the biggest resort in the state, some swear it is the best. The soaring mountains hemming in the town provide a scenic backdrop for a town that has "retained its old-timey small-town feel". Waterfalls entice the explorer. Quaint shops invite browsing, or you can take the gondola up to the ski area for hiking.

And biking! Though it is renowned for mountain biking, road bikes and roller blades are also useful here. A paved trail runs from the east edge of town (Davis St) to the main highway, 3.3 miles of rural riding. Below you the San Miguel River meanders toward town, cutting through green meadows dotted with cows (and a few condos). The path stays level, with only one hill just outside town. The near-vertical mountains flanking you are especially breathtaking at sunset, when the sun's low rays paint the hillsides red.

The trail is currently maintained by volunteers, so any

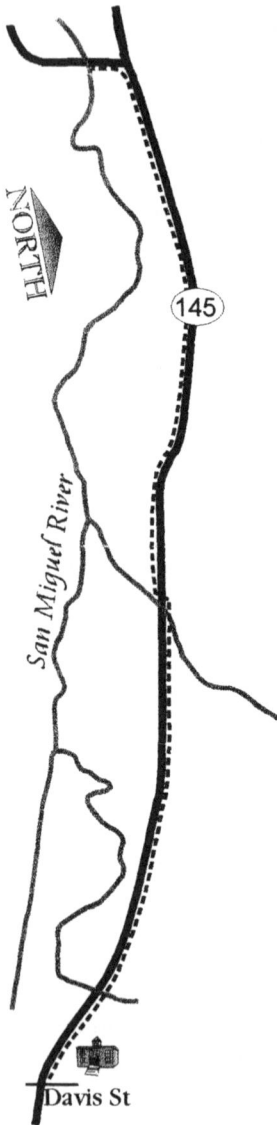

NORTH

145

San Miguel River

Davis St

needed repairs may take a little time. Considering the area it's in, problems that it suffers may be unique. One problem in early 1999: a beaver dam on the river backed up the water, flooding the path. Wetlands laws prevented people from just going in and knocking down the dam!

Plans for this area are indeed grand. Officials project this trail to eventually run fifty miles to Ouray. The San Juan Bikeway will travel through some of the most spectacular mountain scenery in the state. What a day that will be!

WHAT ELSE:

Telluride is the major resort in the San Juans. Every year it hosts festivals throughout the summer, attracting large numbers of tourists. It offers plenty of restaurants and lodging, and campgrounds are available inside or outside of town. Bicycles can be rented in town.

TRAIL:	*Uncompahgre River / Ridgway*
DISTANCE:	*appr. 3.5 miles to reservoir*
SURFACE:	*mostly dirt/crushed gravel*
DIFFICULTY:	*moderate – hilly country*

The San Juan Mountains are recognized as among Colorado's most beautiful – jagged peaks, spectacular wilderness, mountain passes dotted with abandoned mines. The highways running through the region have been named a Scenic Byway, the San Juan Skyway. With luck, they will soon have a companion – the San Juan Bikeway.

BLM and Forest Service officials and representatives from Ouray and San Miguel counties have developed a master plan for a trail that will run for fifty miles through this scenic paradise. Connecting Ouray, Ridgway, and Telluride, the trail will be a crown jewel in Colorado's inventory of bike paths. Another branch will head north from Ridgway, connecting to Montrose. Officials have completed a feasibility study of the main route, and identified options for each stretch of the route.

One piece of this grand path currently exists. Running between Ridgway Town Park and Ridgway Reservoir, it follows the Uncompahgre River as it snakes north. Currently the trail is not continuous. However, backers of the trail have won a ten-year battle with CDOT to finish the last ½ mile, and they expect to open the missing link in summer 1999.

For the lower portion of the trail, leave from the Ridgway Town Park in mid-town, north of CO62. A concrete trail heads out of town, paralleling a dirt road until it hits open space. After crossing the river on a historic bridge trestle, it turns to gravel as it enters BLM land. This area contains covered picnic tables, fishing spots, and a pond used for nesting by herons, bluebirds, and other wildlife. (Please – if you bring a dog here, keep him leashed!)

The trail uses a boardwalk to cross over wetlands along the river, giving you more chances to mingle with nature. Savor the

Ridgway
Reservoir

550

NORTH

Uncompahgre River

Ridgway

62

moment, because you're about to leave the riverbed. At mile 1.2 the trail joins a steep dirt road and climbs back toward US550. The distance on the road is short, but the dirt may make it hard (especially for skinny-tires) to find traction. I had to walk my road bike.a

Before hitting the highway, the trail parts from the road (1.3). Now it runs between a split rail fence and US550, with great views of the San Juans to the south. This portion of the trail ends at mile 1.9, but the connection should be open this summer. At that time it will link up with the rest of the path to the reservoir and state park. Once there, another seven miles of trails weave through the park.

Though a trail extension to Ouray is still in the planning stages, a declared multi-purpose trail does now connect Ridgway to its better-known neighbor. At the south end of Lena St in Ridgway, county road 23 heads into the canyon, linking up with county road 17 to deliver the rider to Ouray. Don't worry about the fact that auto traffic can share the road – most cars chose the quicker US550. Horses and other bikers find this a scenic (and unhurried) alternative.

WHAT ELSE:

Ridgway is a very small, with only a few services available. Camping is available at the reservoir, and nearby Ouray has most services (including bike rentals) that the adventurer needs.

TRAIL:	*Uncompahgre River / Montrose*
DISTANCE:	*4.0 (path) + 0.6 (street) miles*
SURFACE:	*paved, concrete*
DIFFICULTY:	*easy to moderate*

Sometimes, close is good enough.

Some might say that Montrose is only 'close': Close to the grandeur of the Black Canyon of the Gunnison National Monument. Close to the beauty and backcountry of rugged San Juan Mountains. Close to the fishing, hiking, and orchards of Paonia and Hotchkiss. Close to Telluride and Ouray.

When it comes to bicycling, Montrose doesn't settle for 'close'. A network of paved trails weave through the Midwestern-type town, and plans are afoot to connect the town with Ridgway thirty miles to the south.

The newest trails spin off from Baldridge Park, off Rio Grande Ave south of Colorado Ave. Cross the Uncompahgre River on the footbridge and switchback up the bluff to Baldridge. After climbing the barren hillside (as of late 1998, crews were planting the newly developed area), expansive views greet you. The wind may greet you, too – it's very exposed. The trail currently runs 1.2 miles total, then follow it back to the park.

On the river's west side, the trail also meanders downstream. The area is left wild, with trees adding to the Midwestern flavor. It doesn't take long to explore, running only 0.6 or 0.8 miles (the path forks at 0.5).

To connect with the rest of the town, stay on the east bank of the river. The path running through the park soon curves east, reaching city streets at the waterpark at Colorado and Rio Grande (0.6). Just to the south on Rio Grande, boards let you cross the railroad tracks onto Columbia Way. Take that street (which becomes 12th St) 0.5 miles across US550 (Townsend Ave) to the Montrose Arroyo.

The Montrose Arroyo Trail winds through the heart of the

NORTH

city. At times it dumps onto city streets, at other times the surface is in poor shape from frost heaves. For skaters, the trails in Holly Park are recommended. Bikers can take the trail 1.5 miles northwest, passing through several neighborhoods and ending in the parks off Nevada Ave north of Main St (US50). Cross that busy road on Junction Ave, but remember there is no traffic signal.

A trail also runs south from town along the Uncompahgre River. I have not had the opportunity to scout this concrete trail.

WHAT ELSE:

Montrose is best known as a gateway to Black Canyon of the Gunnison National Monument. The area offers lodging, camping, and restaurants, but is not considered a resort.

TRAIL:	*Colorado River / Grand Junction*
DISTANCE:	*7.2 (path) + 5.3 (street) miles*
SURFACE:	*paved, concrete*
DIFFICULTY:	*easy – moderate traffic on city streets*

Early pioneers in today's western Colorado, noting the area's low rainfall, settled near the rivers. The major waterway in the area, aptly named the Grand River, drew its share of homesteaders. Many of them took land near the junction of that river with the Gunnison River, and named their settlement 'Grand Junction'.

Today that town has grown into western Colorado's largest city. The river, renamed the Colorado River in 1921, gives the area character, a meandering ribbon of blue winding through the neighborhoods and orchards of the Grand Valley. Parks along the river open it to recreation. A paved trail follows the waterway at different points, and a cadre of volunteers patrol it, providing help for flat tires or providing information. Eventually, the trail will run from Loma to Island Acres State Park east of Palisade.

At the current time, the trail is broken up into three unconnected sections. The Corn Lake section runs through Colorado River State Park; Watson Island section lies just south of downtown, and Blue Heron covers the western sector. (In summer 1999, the city plans to open a link connecting the Blue Heron and Watson Island sections.)

Corn Lake can be accessed through the state park off 32 Rd (CO141). The trail runs 2.0 miles by ponds reclaimed from gravel mining, ending at 30 Rd. The riverside area is wild, riparian woodland, though homes and businesses lie not too far to the north. The river has cut a swath through some bluffs, exposing shallow cliffs.

You can access Watson Island by parking at the Botanic Gardens (take 7th St south through downtown to its end), or ride to it from Corn Lake: 0.5 miles north on 30 Rd, 1.0 mile west

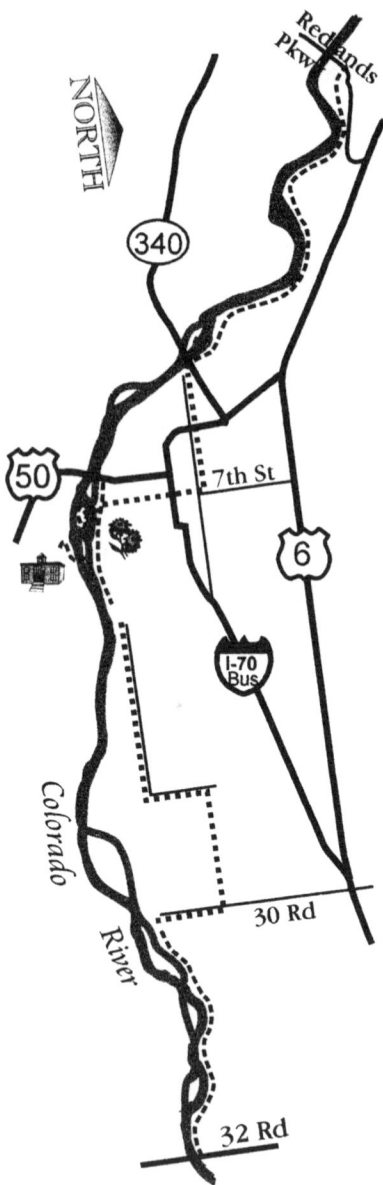

(left) on D Rd, 0.5 miles south (left) on 29 Rd, and 1.5 miles west (right) on C½ Rd. The trail begins where C½ ends at 27½ Rd. a

From 27½, the trail runs west through a wide exposed area with the river south and industry just north. Old Mill Bridge, a new addition, branches off at 0.2 miles to cross the river, climb the bluff, and end at Orchard Mesa School (length 0.4 mile). The main trail continues west, reaching the Botanic Garden (1.0) and Watson Island (1.2). A side trail explores the island, looping 0.6 miles through the woods. Stop and take a break, looking for wildlife.

Return to the Botanic Gardens. To reach Blue Heron, drive to River Rd off Broadway (CO340). To bicycle there, take 7th north 0.7 miles, then Main St west (left) 1.1 miles through the tunnel under the railroad to River Rd, then south one block to pick up the trail.

The Blue Heron is by far the nicest (and longest) stretch of the trail. Fewer businesses interrupt the solitude, while more trees shade you from the sun. The trail follows the river's north banks as it turns toward Fruita. This stretch begins at Riverside Park (Colorado Ave & West Ave), crosses under Broadway, then parallels River Rd. A trailhead on River Rd beckons at mile 1.2; otherwise the trail feels remote until reaching the park and trailhead at Redlands Pkwy (3.2). For a nice break, sit on one of the many park benches and watch the river flow by.

WHAT ELSE:

Grand Junction is the largest city in Western Colorado. Many travelers use the city as a home base while exploring the region. For those interested in dinosaurs, the area is heaven, with museums, laboratories, and exhibits dedicated to the extinct reptiles. Further north, Dinosaur National Monument attracts thousands of visitors every year. One building houses an exposed cliff with hundreds of dinosaur bones sticking out, undisturbed for centuries.

Closer to town, Colorado National Monument looms over the city. The eroded towers and spires display the valleys geologic history. The scenic drive through the park is well worth the effort. East of town, Grand Mesa beckons. Dotted with 200 lakes and thick forests, it offers hiking, fishing, and camping.

Grand Junction is certainly large enough to accommodate most tastes and price ranges for food and lodging. Services (such as bicycle rentals) are available in town.

TRAIL:	*Glenwood Canyon*
DISTANCE:	*15.7 miles*
SURFACE:	*concrete, paved*
DIFFICULTY:	*easy to moderate*

It has been called one of Colorado's engineering marvels, an expensive ($500 million) effort to show that highways and the environment can co-exist. The stretch of I-70 through Glenwood Canyon, the last stretch of the highway completed in Colorado, took years of planning and twelve more to build. The prime directive: to provide access without marring the beauty of the canyon. To achieve that, eight miles of highway was put on viaducts or in tunnels, and rock exposed by blasting was sculpted and stained to match the surroundings. At the same time they put the road in, they constructed a parallel paved trail.

The narrow, steep-walled canyon was never a historic thruway. Native Americans shunned it, preferring to travel over the flat-topped mountains. Pioneer railroaders first conquered the defile in 1891, followed soon by road crews. The first dirt road cost $3000, half the cost of the entire road from Denver to Grand Junction. Early travelers gaped at the scenery, a shady escape from the high plains to the east.

Today the scenery can be enjoyed at a leisurely pace, on the paved trail that runs the length of the canyon. Running at times along the old US6, at times beside – or under – the freeway, the path immerses you in the sights, smells, and sounds of the river. (Beware too much of an immersion – the path lies low enough that the river should flood it every five years!)

The trail can be accessed from either end, or from any of the four rest stops in the canyon. From Glenwood Springs, it starts at the mouth of the canyon, at River St near 6th St. Follow the road east past the Yampah Spa and Vapor Caves, and through the gates onto a wide asphalt strip – the old highway – squeezed between I-70 and the canyon walls. At 1.0 miles a

6th St

River St

Colorado R

to Denver

70

short, sharp hill ends in a narrow bridge over the freeway.

Back on the old road, you can forget about the interstate as you curve around Horseshoe Bend. Towering cliffs and still forests transport you back to earlier times. Too soon, though, traffic noise intrudes again as the trail turns into the main road through No Name, CO (1.8). The houses only last for half a mile as you conquer the trail's biggest hill, cresting (2.3) at the exit for the No Name rest area.

Turn right onto the path and coast downhill back to the water's edge. Pass through a high-water gate at mile 2.8 (if high water hasn't closed it), and pedal below I-70 close to the water. Keep an eye out for rafters! They like to put in at Grizzly Creek, a rest area and park (5.1) worth a short stop. Interpretive signs talk about fish and bats, and the highway behind you.

Follow the trail east, and you soon find yourself under the elevated highway. Kayakers have adopted this stretch of the river as their own; watch them play in the whitewater as you work your way up to the Shoshone power station, where they put in. The trail here weaves through the parking area before it regains the river's edge. After a short lonely stretch, you reach the Hanging Lake rest area (9.6).

The trail here has its greatest crowds, travelers walking to the Hanging Lake Trailhead (10.2). This dirt trail, gaining nearly a thousand feet in one mile, ends at a secluded turquoise lake surrounded by greenery. And the freeway is nowhere in sight! If you can secure your bike or roller blades, it's worth a side trip.

Past Hanging Lake the trail traffic drops significantly. The river has mellowed out, and the woods encroach. At 12.4 miles the trail veers into thick woods to cross over French Creek, then crosses back under the road to reach Bair Ranch rest stop (13.4). The canyon finally opens at mile 15.0, then dives under the road again to reach the eastern terminus (15.7). This trailhead can be reached by taking the Dotsero exit from I-70, and heading west two miles on the north side frontage road.

Now comes the ride back along the trail. Though you gained 100' on your eastbound ride, you can't just coast back. Headwinds will likely make your trek back just as strenuous.

WHAT ELSE:

While not one of Colorado's noted resorts, Glenwood Springs has attracted visitors for years to their hot springs and vapor caves. As such, they offer a variety of restaurants and lodging. Camping is available, as are bike rentals.

SUMMIT & EAGLE COUNTIES

Summit and Eagle Counties, located an hour west of Denver on I-70, are best known as Colorado's winter playground. Every winter weekend, throngs of people escape the metro area for the some of the nation's best-known skiing in Vail, Beaver Creek, Breckenridge, Copper Mountain, Keystone, and Arapahoe Basin.

But the land is far from a one-season destination. Sailing, hiking, fishing, mountain biking, camping and other activities draw vacationers throughout the warmer months. For road bikers, the area offers something special – one of the most extensive network of off-street paths outside of Denver or Colorado Springs.

From US24 exit at Minturn to Keystone resort on US6, the cyclist can pedal over 45 miles on paved paths or city streets designated as bike routes. The trails connect all the towns in Summit County with the major resort of Vail. If you're looking for a leisurely ride alongside Dillon Lake or a grueling test over Vail Pass, this is the place to come!

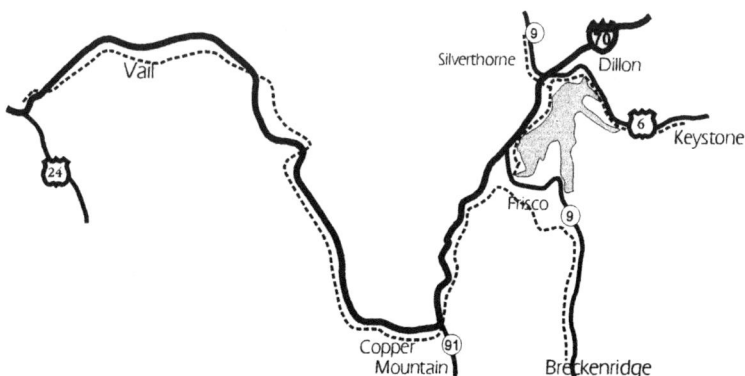

TRAIL: *Gore Creek / Vail*
DISTANCE: *5.7 (path) + 6.2 (street) miles*
SURFACE: *paved*
DIFFICULTY: *moderate – steep on east end; easy otherwise*

What comes to mind when you think of the explorers of the Colorado Rockies? French trappers, looking for beaver? A hard life of solitude, with none of the creature comforts? While that may describe most of the cases, exceptions did happen.

Lord Gore, a wealthy baronet from Ireland in the 1850's, exemplified the opposite case. Eager to try his skills on a three-year hunting expedition in the wilds of America, he assembled a hunting army. His entourage included nearly 50 men, one hundred horses, four dozen hunting dogs, twenty-two wagons and carts, prostitutes, a carpeted silk tent, a fur-lined commode, and three months' worth of trade whiskey (a mixture of 180-proof grain alcohol and red pepper). Nothing like getting back to nature!

Mountain man Jim Bridger guided him into the Rockies, where they visited the Vail area. While there, his party shot every elk, buffalo, and deer in range. Lord Gore took a few trophies, but left thousands of animals to rot. (Later in his trip, Indians had enough of his antics. A war party surrounded Gore and his men in the Black Hills, took their horses, supplies, and clothes, and left them wandering naked in the wild.)

Today Vail still attracts people longing for adventure without sacrificing comfort. Situated along I-70, it fills a vital link in the state's (and nation's) transportation network. It also plays a key part in east-to-west bike traffic. From Minturn in the Eagle River Valley, a paved path/bike route runs to the base of Vail Pass, where it connects to trails that run into and through Summit County. As of early 1999, a bicyclist can ride nearly over forty miles to Keystone without leaving the bike path network – the longest in Colorado.

From the east the ride begins at the gate next to the Gore

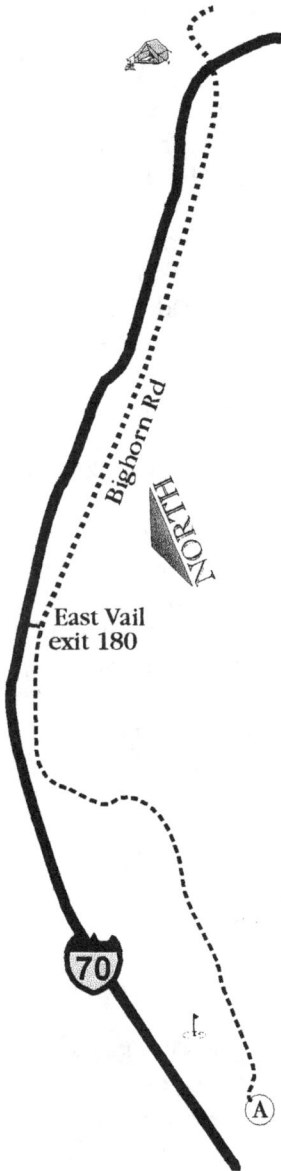

Creek Campground. Follow the old US6 as it dives under the interstate and becomes Bighorn Rd. The slope (steep near the gate) quickly decreases, though it remains downhill through East Vail. Traffic on Bighorn is not heavy, but keep to the marked bike lanes anyway. On either side you pass condos, but nowhere is there a business to be found.

As you near the I-70 exit, a path breaks off to the left (2.4). Now you find yourself in a wild area as you leave East Vail behind. The trail crosses Gore Creek and meanders toward the valley walls, taking you through an area filled with wildflowers in season.

Soon the wild brush gives way to well-manicured grass as you hit the edges of the Vail Golf Club. Watch out for errant golf balls! After navigating switchbacks through another copse of trees, you will cross the golf cart path as you continue to circle the course. The rolling terrain keeps you high enough above Gore Creek to present impressive views of the valley.

The off-street trail ends at mile 4.4, dumping you onto Sunburst Dr ('A' on the maps). Follow the quiet street past elegant condos and (eventually) the golf course until reaching Vail Valley Dr (5.0). A small sign designates the the street as a 'Recreational Path', so take it. More expensive homes and

Bighorn Rd

NORTH

East Vail
exit 180

70

A

(A)

Sunburst Dr.

NORTH

70

Valley Dr.

Vail

exit 176   Vail Rd

Meadow Dr

(B)

golf course holes follow as you wend your way through town.

Across from the Nature Center (5.9), kids play on the soccer fields. (This is another option for parking, if you wish to avoid the steep section near the campground.) A concrete side trail here leads down to Gerald Ford Park & Amphitheater and to tennis courts. Ahead, a side trail at Mill Creek Cir (6.4) provides access to a city park and the chairlifts behind them. The main route continues straight down Valley View across the creek, then turns left on E Meadow Dr.

You have now reached the heart of the town. To your left, the Vail Transportation Center provides the main parking structure for the town. E Meadow turns into a pedestrian mall, with throngs of tourists window shopping, checking out the restaurants, or just relaxing in the mountain sun. Take extra care (or walk your bike) as you work your way down to Vail Rd (6.9).

You share W Meadow Rd with cars again, until reaching the Vail Valley Medical Center (7.1), when the bike trail begins again (map label 'B'). The trail ducks into the woods near the creek, before being shunted by a miniature golf course to the Eagle Bahn gondola (7.4). Want to see the high country? Then grab a ride up the mountain – the gondola runs daily.

28

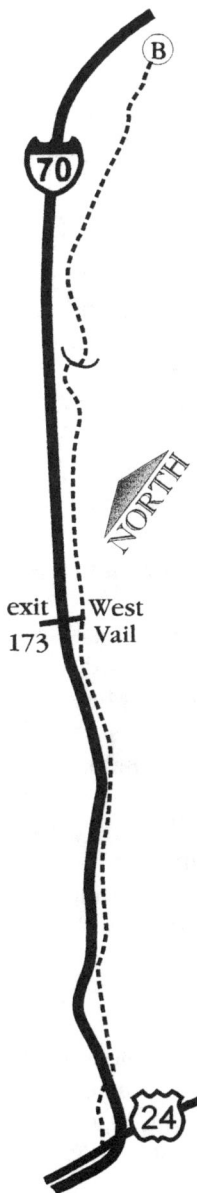

To continue, apply your brakes as you follow the trail down a steep corkscrew between the gondola and the bridge. The trail dips then rises then dips again as it starts to leave Vail behind. When you cross Gore Creek again (7.9), it's hard to believe that you're so close to a major resort. Trees surround you, and anglers ply the creek below.

The feeling doesn't last. You cross the creek again (8.2) and skirt the condo complexes. At mile 8.7 the trail dumps you onto Westhaven St, with no continuation in sight. Jog right a few yards, and the trail resumes where the road bends.

Enjoy one more short stretch of nature before the trail tracks S Frontage Rd, giving you unobstructed views of I-70. Next up is exit 173 off the interstate with its resulting businesses. The trail crosses a traffic circle at the Marriott Streamside (9.8), then joins a bike lane on the frontage road. Follow this to the end, where the canyon narrows (10.9). One last section of trail picks up here, running between the creek and the interstate through the narrow defile. It crosses under I-70 at mile 11.6, looping around to cross over the creek and end (11.9) at the Minturn exit (exit 171).

WHAT ELSE:

The resort of Vail attracts travelers worldwide for its outdoor recreation. Hike, camp, fish, four-wheel, take gondola rides. The area offers many choices in lodging or restaurant, and you can rent bikes in town.

TRAIL:	*East Vail to Vail Pass*
DISTANCE:	*8.7 miles*
SURFACE:	*paved path and old highway*
DIFFICULTY:	*very strenuous – constant steep climb from base*

Once upon a time a middle-aged bicyclist, little tested by mountain riding, agreed to go with friends on their annual Frisco-to-Vail-and-back bike ride. His confidence bolstered by a relatively easy ride up the east side of Vail Pass, he followed them to mid-Vail for a quick lunch before starting the return ride.

The hero of our story started lagging behind as they left East Vail. By the time he reached the gates at Gore Creek Campground his friends were out of sight, far up the trail. Quickly he discovered why cyclists demand three, not two, gears on their front derailleur for mountain cycling. Slowly, with many rests, he reached the tunnel under the freeway – and the steepest portion of the ride.

Totally demoralized (and stranded!) he hauled the bike onto the interstate shoulder and stuck out his thumb. A ride quickly stopped – a car with the distinctive markings of the county sheriff. After calling in to verify that the biker was not an escaped murderer, the deputy offered him a ride to the top of the pass.

On the hilltop, as our hero extracted his bike from the back seat of the sheriff's cruiser, he heard a voice behind him. "That's cheating!" called out a motorcyclist in leather. Spinning around, the cyclist looked at the figure atop his Harley, and exclaimed –

"Dad!?! What the heck are you doing here?" Just out for a weekend ride, it seems. Oh, 'tis such a small world.

As the preceding tale should indicate, this ride (unlike most others in this book) is not an easy jaunt. It involves a longer, steeper climb than the approach from the east. If you're looking for a workout this route excels, with wide pavement (partly

to Vail

along the old US6) and few other bikes to share it with. Just be sure to allow enough time to conquer it!

This route begins at the parking area at the gates at Gore Creek Campground. To get here, exit I-70 at East Vail and follow Bighorn Rd to the end. The trail continues on the old US6, a wide ribbon of asphalt quickly climbing up to the pass. Focus on the scenery as you inch up the road: Trees share the hillsides with meadows. Wildlife rustles through the forests. Below you, Black Gore Creek tumbles downstream.

After covering 3.5 uphill miles, signs direct you into the woods on a side trail (the old road ends just around the bend). A quick downhill takes you across Polk Creek and under I-70 (3.8), where you face the steepest pitch of the ride. Once you climb back to freeway level, the slope lessens ever so slightly. The trail dodges back and forth, now by the interstate, then in a stand of trees, until cutting away at mile 5.7. Now the slope finally moderates as it takes a short detour into the trees. When it exits, it keeps the lesser slope as it runs parallel to (and below) the highway.

Following the extreme pitches of the lower trail, this stretch feels like heaven. The scenery improves as you gain more elevation. Slowly Black Gore Creek rises nearly to your level. The trail levels off as you reach Black Lake #2 (7.0), and climbs only slowly. Soon you regain the old highway (7.5), and pass through the gate keeping out autos (7.7) just before reaching Black Lake #1 (7.8). Stop and catch your breath one last time, watching the

NORTH

to Copper Mtn

people fish. Then tackle the last short stretch of old road, reaching the pass at mile 8.7 – 2000' above the level you started.

Oh, in case you're wondering – I did come back the following year with a new (21-speed) bike. This time I finished the ride, though it took hours. Maybe the key is to start the trip in Vail, hitting this leg when you're fresh ...

TRAIL: *Copper Mountain to Vail Pass*
DISTANCE: *5.7 miles*
SURFACE: *paved*
DIFFICULTY: *strenuous*

Vail Pass is not the highest pass in Colorado. It does not even rank in the top ten.

It is not the highest point along I-70. Eisenhower Tunnel, at 11,158' earns that distinction.

However, Vail Pass is the highest pass (and only one, to the author's knowledge) that has a bike path running over it. At 10,666' above sea level, it may also be the highest paved trail in the state. To get a good workout combined with a feeling of accomplishment, you could do far worse than Vail Pass.

From the east side, I-70 leaves Copper Mountain ski area and climbs up the watershed of West Tenmile Creek. To maintain the desired grades, east- and west-bound lanes were pushed to opposite sides of the canyon, leaving a wild area filled with trees, brush, and a tumbling stream in the center. The bike trail winds it way through this pristine park, surrounding you with nature rather than the smells of exhaust.

Start logging your mileage from the intersection of Copper Road and CO91. Follow Copper Rd west to the signed bike route, then turn left onto Tenmile Cr at the Copper Mountain Resort and Mountain Plaza. Follow the bike signs to the left (0.9), winding through the resort. Watch for the trail to resume on your left (1.1).

As you leave the resort, the trail passes stables. Horseback riding attracts many people, and you may see a group saddling up for a ride. The trail closely follows the creek lined with bushes, and trees press close by.

After passing under the east-bound lanes of I-70, the trail climbs into more open meadows. Even though you are constantly climbing, the slope is not gut-busting (especiallywhen compared to the slope on the west side of the

33

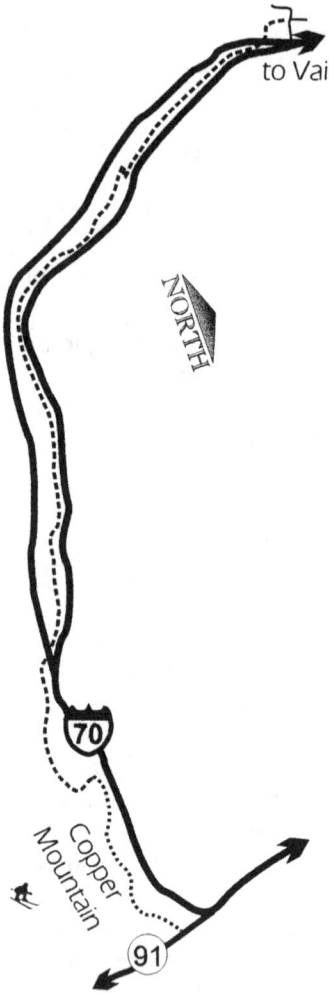

pass). Switchbacks at mile 3.6 and 3.7 may have you gasping for breath, but then the land flattens out and you can see nearly to the pass.

After rolling along the nearly level land of the upper creek, the trail throws another set of switchbacks at you (mile 4.7-5.2). Take heart that you are nearing the end and push onward. The last half-mile to the summit levels off again, letting you catch your breath. After passing back under the interstate, follow the road to the left to reach the pass-top parking lot.

Congratulations! You have climbed nearly 1000' from the base of the mountain. Now you have a great downhill run ahead of you. Take care on the return, though – some of the curves you crawled around while climbing become very sharp at downhill speeds.

While this ride is definitely taxing, most physically fit cyclists should have little real difficulty in reaching the summit. Indeed, summer weekends will find families making the ride. This route does rank as this book's second most strenuous, but beware! The path on the other side is even steeper, losing 2000' to the gates at Gore Creek Campground. If you head that way, be sure to save enough energy to make the climb back up.

TRAIL: *Tenmile Creek / Frisco to Copper Mountain*
DISTANCE: *7.7 miles*
SURFACE: *paved*
DIFFICULTY: *moderate to strenuous*

Even with a trail system as extensive as the one in Summit County, there had to be a starting point, a trail that led the way. Here, the Tenmile Creek Trail wins that honor.

Running from Frisco to Copper Mountain through a narrow canyon, the trail follows an old rail bed. When the railroad gave up, it turned into a county road, and eventually auto traffic was banned. Now the pavement is home to bicyclists, skaters, and people out for a walk through nature.

Though you can start this ride from many points in Frisco, we will trace directions (and distance) from the Frisco Marina and tourist info center, Main St and CO9. Signs direct the rider 1.0 miles through town on a jagged route (described in the writeup for the Breckenridge ride). When 7th Ave ends, turn right on the trail.

You now cruise through a wooded stretch on the edge of Frisco. Some houses break the scenery, and you pass through a city park en route to Tenmile Creek. At mile 2.2 a side bridge provides access to another trailhead, one you may chose to use instead of driving through town. It is accessible from the Main St exit off I-70 (exit 201), on the right immediately east of the interstate.

From here the trail climbs up Tenmile Canyon. The steep sides of the canyon shade it through much of the morning, making it a cool early ride on hot summer days. Though you share the canyon with busy I-70, the traffic is often invisible behind the trees. Unfortunately, the highway noise is more difficult to escape.

The ride gives you a good taste of nature. Aspens line the trail, and the scent of pines fills the air. Flowers add color to the green surrounding, and the creek tumbles against the rocks in

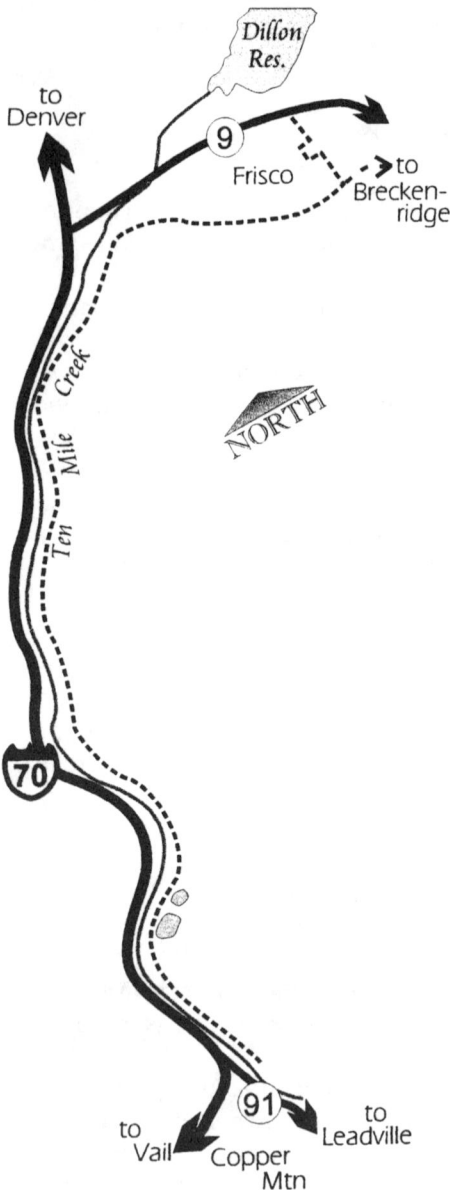

to
Denver

*Dillon
Res.*

(9)

Frisco

> to
Brecken-
ridge

Ten Mile Creek

NORTH

[70]

to
Vail

(91)

Copper
Mtn

to
Leadville

its bed. The steep slopes across the canyon mark the edge of the Eagle's Nest Wilderness Area.

Steadily the trail climbs, with steeper pitches followed by more level terrain. After one stiff rise, you pass a trailside pond (4.2). Its calm waters contrast with the whitewater of the creek on your other side. The slope eases here, letting you catch your breath before the next climb. The trail finally levels off for good at mile 6.2, soon passes another pair of ponds.

Slowly the canyon widens as it enters Wheeler Flats. You may see people wandering through the wetlands area as you near trail's end. After two creek crossings, you reach Wheeler Flats trailhead (7.7) This is a good place to get dropped off if you're only looking for a downhill run into Frisco. If you're itching for a bigger challenge, though, follow the road out to CO91 and cross it onto Copper Rd. Further directions are in the writeup for Copper Mountain to Vail Pass.

WHAT ELSE:

Summit County excels in opportunities for outdoor recreation. Mountain biking, fishing, four-wheeling, golfing, hiking, horseback riding, sailing, and tennis all keep the visitor active. The main towns and resorts in the county all offer the visitor the standard services. Lodging is readily available, from luxury lodges to chains such as Holiday Inn. Restaurants offer food for all price levels, and nightlife abounds. Bicycle rentals and repairs can be had in outlets throughout the area.

TRAIL:	*Blue River / Frisco to Breckenridge*
DISTANCE:	*8.0 (path) + 1.0 (street) miles*
SURFACE:	*paved*
DIFFICULTY:	*easy to moderate*

Borne of a Colorado gold rush in 1860, Breckenridge became the state's first permanent settlement west of the Continental Divide. After naming their village for Vice President John C. Breckinridge, the town fathers grew disgusted by his support of the Confederacy. Their retaliation: changing the first *i* in the town's name to an *e*.

Its early years were typical gold camp, with its share of characters and events. In 1897 miner Tom Groves unearthed 'Tom's Baby', the largest (13 pounds) gold nugget ever discovered. 'Captain' Sam Adams found his fame by forming the Breckenridge Navy. He talked locals into giving him four boats and a crew of ten to float down the Blue River to the Colorado River and on to the Pacific. The attempt failed miserably, and he took leave of the town.

The Blue River still figures prominently here. Fishermen ply the stream, and cyclists pedal alongside it. The paved trail that follows it downstream connects to the system running through the county, providing access to the sports of Dillon Lake.

This trail has one end in the town of Frisco. From the Frisco Marina, the route runs a crooked, well-posted route through town before going off-street. Follow Main St one block west from CO9 to 7th Ave, go left two blocks to Granite St, right one block to 6th Ave, and left two blocks to its end. Head left one block on Frisco St to 7th (0.5 miles) and turn right, following that to the end (1.0). From here, the trail takes off into the woods.

Head left on the trail. Only a few houses interrupt the wilderness feeling; otherwise you share the land with trees, streams, and other bikers and bladers. The highway comes into view briefly at mile 2.3 before the trail turns, tracing a roller-coaster route over small hills, curving wildly through the trees.

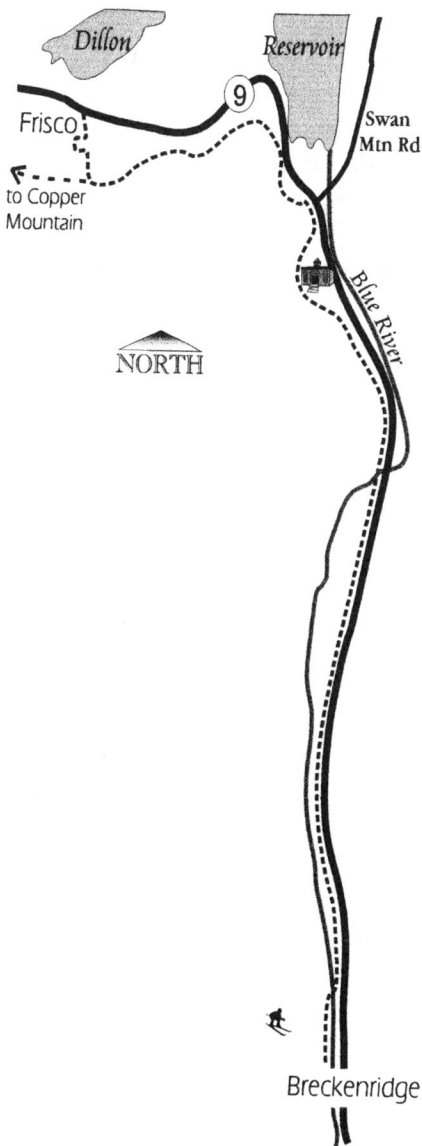

Due to blind curves, make sure to check your speed.

A sharp curve (3.2 miles) puts you next to Hwy 9, then you veer away to follow the edge of a field around Summit High School. Soon the trail settles into paralleling the highway (4.3) as it speeds toward Breckenridge, often filled with bike and roller blade traffic. A trailhead (parking only) lies on Gateway Rd/Rd 950 (5.9), just before you cross over the river (6.0).

Though the auto traffic to your left ruins the solitude, the views of mountain peaks and glimpses of fishermen in the Blue River make it a worthwhile ride. Just do your best to ignore the gravel operations flanking the road until mile 7.5.

After passing a small rest stop (table and bench) at mile 7.1, you begin to approach Breckenridge. The river hides behind thick bushes, and a pullout (8.7) gives a great view onto the ski area. The trail passes under three streets before ending at Watson Rd (9.0) on the edge of downtown. You can stop and window shop, pick up supplies, or eat before heading back for a (mostly downhill) run back to Frisco along the same path.

WHAT ELSE:

See the writeup under Tenmile Creek.

TRAIL:	*Lake Dillon Loop / Frisco - Dillon - Frisco*
DISTANCE:	*11.5 (path) + 7.0 (street) miles*
SURFACE:	*paved*
DIFFICULTY:	*strenuous on Swan Mtn Rd, else easy to moderate*

Water – or the lack of it – played an important part in the settlement of Colorado and the West. When it didn't flow where the power players wanted it to, they simply dammed and redirected it. As Denver grew into a major city, it needed more and more water for its burgeoning population, and leaders looked further afield to supply those demands. When they saw the flows of three streams – the Blue and Snake Rivers and Tenmile Creek – being allowed to escape downstream to the Colorado, they deigned to stop it. The result was Dillon Reservoir. 'Twas only a minor problem to tunnel under the Continental Divide and deliver it to the city.

Once the project completed in the early 1960's, Dillon Reservoir became the recreational centerpiece of the county. Fishers, boaters, and campers all come to the lake to play, often enjoying cool lake breezes on hot summer weekends. For the more mobile visitor a bike route circles the lake, with over 60% on paved off-street bikeways.

A convenient starting point is the Frisco Marina, Main St at CO9. The trail starts from Main St, heading north through a stand of trees then next to highway 9 as it crosses Tenmile Creek. It quickly leaves the road, climbing a short rise before rolling east above the water's edge. On the left you pass Summit School (0.8 miles) and a running track before curving away from the lake. After leaving the track, the trail winds through a thicket with no signs of town visible.

At 1.5 miles the land opens into a brushy meadow, with houses ahead. Turn left when you hit the street (1.8), right on Lakepoint Dr (signed) and right on Divide (not signed) to hit the trail again (2.0). It takes you into another meadow, then into trees. Islands dot the lake in front of you.

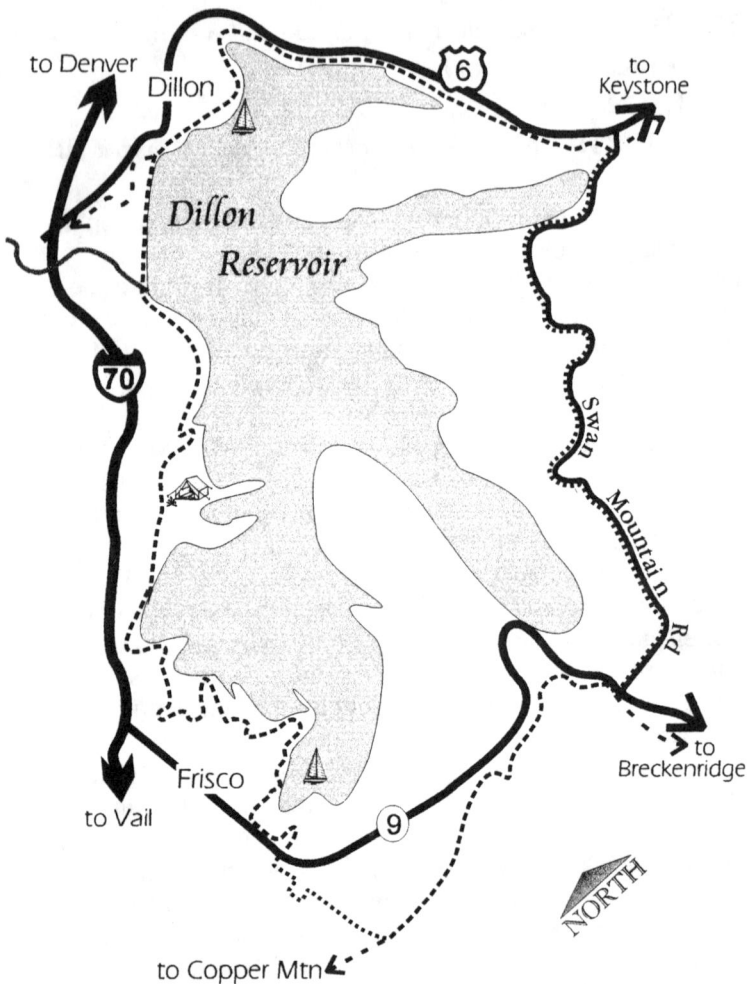

Join the shoulder of Dam Rd (2.7) for a short haul before the trail splits off again. The area here is heavily wooded, and small hills offer a slight workout for the biker. A signed trail to restrooms offers a break at mile 3.2, or you can forego it. Ahead, the trail passes a campground, then spurs to an osprey viewing area (3.9) and historic view (4.2) branch to the right.

The trail next joins Dam Rd on a marked lane (4.3). Soon a guardrail protects you from traffic (4.8) as you shadow the road over the dam. Once on the other side (6.0), the trail quickly branches (6.1). The left fork runs to Dillon and Silverthorne – see that writeup for more information.

Continue straight, traversing a greenbelt until the next trail fork (6.2). This time the straight-ahead option passes signs telling you to dismount to walk your bike through the marina park. Instead, take the left branch, which dumps you onto Lodgepole St. Follow that until mile 6.6, when the trail reappears. Follow it off the bluff to where it dumps onto another side street (6.9). Take that street out, and turn right on Tenderfoot St (not signed, but it is the only street). The trail begins again at mile 7.4.

The surrounding land here is filled with brush and dirt. Above you is US6; below you, the lake. Images of sailboats cutting through the water may break the monotony of this stretch, but little else catches the eyes. Soon enough the lake ends (8.6). Stay on the paved trail as it crosses the dirt road, then skirt trees on the hillside as you parallel US6 below you. When you cross the side road to the pricey estates (9.2), look for the trail to continue close to the highway.

Suddenly the lake reappears! This is the Snake River arm, hidden before now behind a small mountain. Take the trail to the water's end, then grab the right fork (9.9) to reach Swan Mountain Rd (10.0).

To achieve a loop trip, you must travel over Swan Mountain Rd. There is no shoulder on the road. Traffic is light, but it is there. As the name implies, it climbs above the lake. If this does not appeal to you, you may return along the bike trail. If you choose to continue, you will be rewarded with great views of the lake and a sense of accomplishment. While not the most strenuous ride in this book (it lags behind the rides to Vail Pass), it does rank #3.

The road wastes little time in gaining elevation. During the first climb, you can distract yourself by looking down on the lake or across it to the pricey estates you bypassed earlier. After a bend the slope lessens, but you continue to climb. After working up a good sweat, you reach the crest (12.9) at Sapphire Point overlook. Take a restroom break if needed, or take a short hike to the overlook. The views from this elevation are indeed impressive.

The downhill is over quickly. At mile 14.9 signs announce a trail to Frisco on the right, but it shortly ends on the shoulder of CO9 (15.2). Cross the road and join the Frisco-Breckenridge trail (mile 3.2 on that route – see that writeup). Follow the instructions on that ride to return to the Frisco Marina (18.5) and complete your loop.

WHAT ELSE:
See the writeup under Tenmile Creek.

TRAIL:	*Connections to Keystone & Silverthorne*
DISTANCE:	*6.3 miles*
SURFACE:	*concrete, paved*
DIFFICULTY:	*easy – some traffic on city streets*

The trail system in Summit County connects all the towns and resorts. The Blue River Trail connects Frisco to Breckenridge. Copper Mountain ties in to Frisco via the Tenmile Creek Trail. Dillon is a short run on the Lakeside Trail away from Frisco.

The county's largest town, Silverthorne, lies just downstream of Dillon Lake. A trail along the lower portion of the Blue River, combined with a route along city streets, provides access between the town and the lake. To the east, Keystone occupies a spot upstream. When the Dillon Lake Loop trail ends at Swan Mountain Road, a branch follows the Snake River (no, not that Snake River) into town.

This route can be started in the town on either end, or begun in the middle. Perhaps the best place to catch the trail is at the lakefront parking by the Dillon Marina. To get there, take US6 to Chief Colorow St and follow that to its end.

Since the middle portion of this route is described in the Dillon Lake Loop writeup, this section will describe the paths that link that route to the loop trail. Your total mileage will vary depending on how far you follow the path into Silverthorne, but will top out at 10.1 miles one-way.

Connection to Keystone – from the Swan Mountain Rd fork (mile 9.9 of the loop trip), bear left and veer back toward US6. Cross the intersection of US6 and Swan Mountain at mile 0.2, and follow the trail as it runs between the highway and a row of houses. After crossing the next side road (0.6) you enter a new real estate development. On either side of you lies a new golf course (which was being installed when this ride was scouted, September 1998).

Past the golf course (1.2), large condos carve out yards on

45

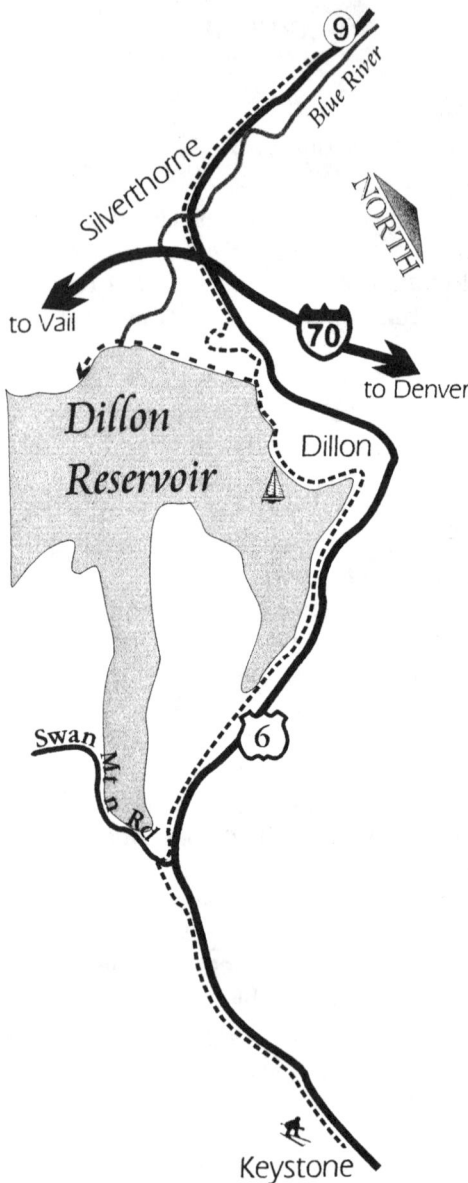

your left, while the Snake River – more a nice brook than a river – flows to your right. The trail branches at mile 1.4, with the right fork leading to a neighborhood. Pay close attention to this spot! On your return trip, the side trail over the bridge may look like the main path. Instead, look for the sign that says "Snake River path to Summit Cove".

Soon the trail veers from the creek (2.1) to enter an area covered with brush and flowers. After a short spin through the greenery, the trail dumps onto a local road (2.4). 'Dismount' signs greet you as you walk your bike behind businesses and then through a pedestrian strip by a pond. The simple shops lining the pond, along with the crowds milling about (and maybe a paddleboat on the water) lend a European feel to the scene.

You can mount the bike again at mile 2.6, leaving the pond to ride past the Mountain House and by a park with exercise equipment. Past the park, the trail joins an access road (2.8) which takes it across the river. Take a left on the business road, and follow into Keystone Village (3.2).

Connection to Silverthorne – the Silverthorne trail splits from the loop trail just before the lakeside park (6.1 in the loop writeup). Take the fork to the left, dropping under Dam Rd and crossing the old bike path. After winding underneath the dam, the trail dumps onto E Anemone Tr (0.4).

From here the trail uses city streets and sidewalks to reach Silverthorne. The easiest route is turn right on Anemone, then pass through the Dillon Factory Stores (0.7) en route to catching the sidewalk on US6 (do not cross the highway). Follow this sidewalk under the freeway (1.0).

After crossing the Blue River and leaving the main business area (1.3) the sidewalk becomes more of a trail. However, it continues closely following Blue River Pkwy/CO9. A traffic light at 6th St (1.8) marks the end of most of the town's businesses. The trail does continue on until ending at Golden Eagle Rd (3.1), but it seems pointless. With no notable scenery, why ride it (unless you're staying out there)?

WHAT ELSE:
See the writeup under Tenmile Creek.

MOUNTAINS

The Rocky Mountains give Colorado its character. A spiny backbone stretching north and south, the range dominates scenery, bedevils traffic, affects weather, and draws a steady stream of tourists.

This region has always drawn people for the riches found there. First came the beaver pelts, attracting trappers. Later fortune seekers discovered its mineral treasures, sparking a population boom. Water and lumber continue to fuel economies. In the late 20th century, though, recreation has become a major player.

No longer do any mountain towns limit their draw to winter sports. Hiking, camping, horseback riding, kayaking, and other ventures help keep visitors' interest high year-round. Multi-use trails are booming, with more planned for the upcoming years. Perhaps the most ambitious plans come from Grand County, where the master plan calls for a trail linking Berthoud and Rabbit Ears Passes – 80 miles apart!

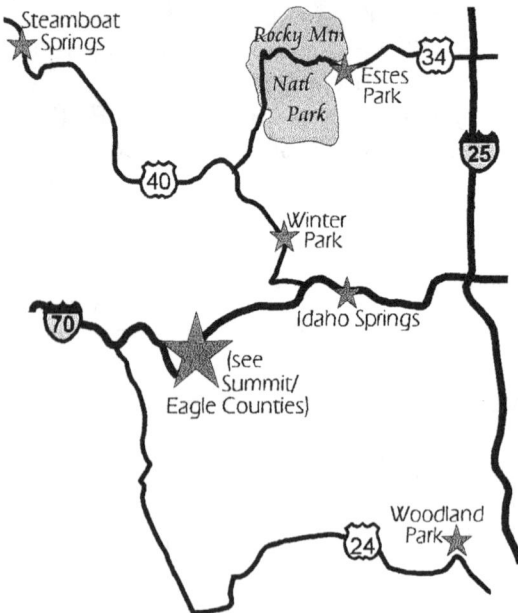

TRAIL: *Yampa River / Steamboat Springs*
DISTANCE: *4.7 - 6.1 miles one-way, depending on options*
SURFACE: *paved*
DIFFICULTY: *easy, with a moderate hill on Mt Werner Dr*

Steamboat Springs was named in 1865 by French trappers riding along the Yampa River. They heard a chugging sound which they mistook for a steamboat. Investigation found a hot spring chugging along, churning hot water into the river. The spring continued to sound off until 1908, when railroad workers blasted out a rock chamber and silenced it.

Other springs join Steamboat in the area's thermal play. Strawberry Park Hot Springs offers rock-lined pools for a hot soak in natural surroundings. Iron Spring, Soda Spring, Heart Spring and others bubble forth inside city limits. In Lincoln Park, Sulfur Springs flows at 70°, emitting a rotten-egg smell that has caused some locals to dub the area 'Fart Park'. Those in the know swear that when the smell gets real bad, start celebrating – a big snowfall is on the way.

The trail running through the city starts in Lincoln Park, at Lincoln Ave/US40 and 13th St. Head south at the park's edge, crossing under 13th and passing by the library. You may see fishermen in the river – spin and bait casters do quite well. Follow the path over the river (0.5 miles) and under the railroad tracks via Howelsen Tunnel.

To your right lie municipal ballfields and Howelsen Hill, the town's noted ski jump hill. Though Steamboat Springs is still best-known (and rightly so) for its superb skiing, the summer belongs to softball. Tournaments pitting teams from across the country happen nearly every weekend. Next door to Howelsen Hill, the Rodeo Grounds draws crowds every Friday and Saturday night.

Follow the trail across 5th St (0.8) and through a tunnel onto an island splitting the Yampa River. The lush island is over quickly, and a bridge dumps you back onto the east bank. On

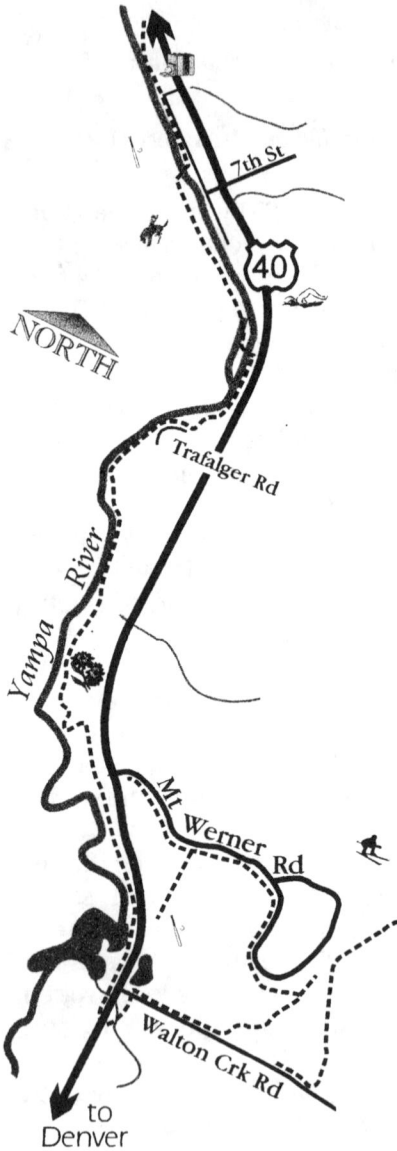

hot summer days the traffic under the bridge is heavier than that on the trail, with inner tubers floating down the stream. Several outfitters in town rent tubes, shuttling floaters upstream to the put-in.

The next short stretch stays semi-wild, with no road crowding the trail. At 1.6 miles the trail turns right onto Trafalger Dr, but promptly turns back onto the path. After passing a few houses the trail runs along the edge of a new park, with ballfields and soccer fields for organized sport. Across the river, forested slopes provide a green background. Noise from the river hides the sound of traffic from the never-distant US40.

If you have time, stroll through the botanic gardens (2.2). A new attraction adjacent to the trail, it has walking paths, a pond, and several theme gardens. Ahead on the trail lies the Fish Creek modular homes, then by a lumber yard, fishing pond, and more native flora.

50

By the time you reach the Mt Werner Rd (3.3), the steep slopes to the west have become rolling hills. Hills to the east now grow steeper, marking the ski area. Continue straight past the tuber's put-in, running between the river and the highway.

The trail passes under US40 at mile 4.1, and then splits. To the right the path crosses a bridge before turning to gravel and ending at mile 4.6. (Plans are underway to extend this leg a bit further.) Instead, head left, cross Walton Creek Rd, and pass by Casey's Pond to reach more softball fields. Past the field the path reforms on your left and takes you to Mt Werner Rd (4.7).

Time for another decision. If you wish to return now to Lincoln Park, take the path to the left. It follows the road back to Mt Werner Rd stop sign after passing under the highway (5.2). To explore the base of the ski area, turn right instead. Follow the sidewalk trail uphill to mile 5.2, and stop to enjoy the view. Below you the tennis center, open fields, and a much-photographed barn spread out at the base of the hill.

At Eagle Ridge Dr the trail leaves the road, dropping quickly to the Village Center. Another junction greets you at mile 5.4, providing more options. You may go left, then turn left on Village Dr, and right on Apres Ski Ln to reach another paved path between condos. A left here takes you to the mountain gondola offering sightseeing rides during the summer. A right on this path takes you on a short climb behind condos and fields, ending at Walton Creek Rd (5.8). Turn right here to go down Walton Creek Rd, reaching Eagle Ridge Dr/Whistler Rd at mile 6.1.

If you took a right turn at the junction at mile 5.4, the trail follows the creek down Eagle Ridge in front of a large condo complex. It merges with the path in the above paragraph when it reaches Walton Creek Rd (5.7), saving you nearly a half-mile. Follow Walton Creek Rd down another 0.3 miles to reach Casey's Pond, and then choose which route to return on.

WHAT ELSE:

Steamboat is a popular resort, far enough from Denver to

51

'get away from it all', yet close enough to reach on the weekends. Though skiing put in on the map, the crowds don't abate during the summer season. Perhaps the busiest weekend occurs in mid-July, during the Rainbow Weekend. Art in the Park complements a hot-air balloon rodeo, where balloonists attempt to negotiate their craft close enough to a mock steer to rope it. The Strings in the Mountains Chamber Music Ensemble provide a score to the whole affair.

The standard outdoor activities are all offered here, as well as some not often seen elsewhere. Inner tubing down the Yampa River attracts scores of people every hot summer day, so many that the outfitters now regulate how many people they rent tubes to on the weekends. At Clark, 25 miles north of the Springs, the Elk River Valley Llama Company offers one- to five-day llama trekking adventures. And, of course, hot springs invite you in for a soak after a strenuous day of adventuring.

Being a resort town, all expected amenities are available. Several shops in town offer full-service mountain bike rentals and repairs.

TRAIL:	*Lake Estes / Estes Park*
DISTANCE:	*3.8 miles*
SURFACE:	*concrete, pavement*
DIFFICULTY:	*easy, moderate on east end*

Estes Park has long held an attraction to humans as well as wildlife. Indians considered the area sacred, and Arapahos climbed Longs Peak to trap eagles. F. O. Stanley popularized the resort with his Stanley Hotel (inspiration for Stephen King's *The Shining*), and Rocky Mountain National Park just to the west draws millions of people every year. The wildlife wander into town regularly – it's no surprise to find bugling elk on the golf course in the fall.

During the summer throngs of people arrive to wander through the shops, enjoy the festivals, and explore the National Park. Lake Estes offers boating and fishing, and a trail that circles it. The lake park complex is easily reached from the Visitor Center on US34 immediately northeast of US36.

From the Visitor Center, head east along the paved trail toward the golf course. When the trail branches, take the left fork past the power station. You promptly enter the Matthews-Reese Bird Sanctuary, a thickly forested rest spot for our avian friends. By the time the lake comes into view, you leave the sanctuary and cross the Thompson River (0.4 miles). Signs warn to "watch for errant golf balls."

After passing the park at Fisherman's Nook (0.6), the trail squeezes between the lake and cliffs. The area is the lake's most remote, though you pass platforms for anglers to access the fishing grounds. When the cliffs recede, you enter the marina area (1.2) with picnic tables, horseshoe pits, and crowds of people.

The trail leaves the lake and promptly branches. Turning left would take you back to the Visitor's Center – but why would you want to ride by the side of US34? Turn back instead, or take the right fork, which dumps you onto the shoulder of (busy)

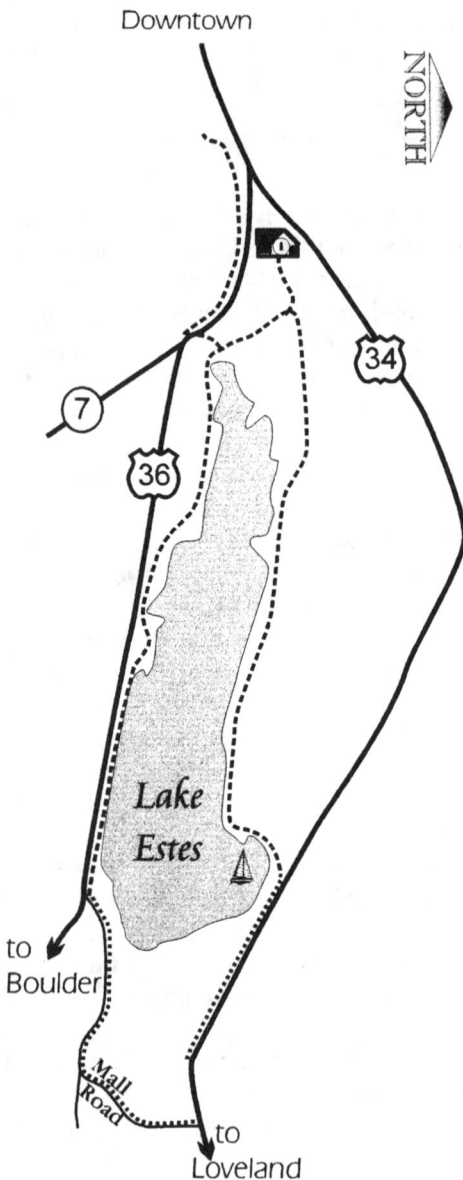

NORTH

Downtown

34

7

36

Lake
Estes

to
Boulder

Mall
Road

to
Loveland

US34. Follow the highway past the go-kart/bumperboat/mini-golf park until reaching Mall Rd (1.9), your first chance to turn right. Do so, and follow the side road as it drops and then rises.

The trail reappears before you hit US36. Be careful on the first stretch – ripples in the concrete and occasional sand could cause problems if you get moving too fast. The slope quickly levels out as you cruise between the highway and the lake, then the highway and lake part (3.0) as the trail runs through parking areas, picnic tables and fishermen. The power plant marks the end of the loop (3.8), with the Visitor Center dead ahead.

An option at this point is to follow the side trail up from the power plant to the road, crossing US36 and CO7 at the light.

The trail shadows US36 across the Thompson River (0.4), then runs between downtown businesses and the river until ending at a plaza (0.7). This stretch is tough to ride, since it is normally crowded with pedestrians. However, it does provide convenient access to downtown.

WHAT ELSE:

Estes Park is best known as a gateway to Rocky Mountain National Park. One of the ten most popular National Park sites (and one of the most crowded), it offers a superb Rocky Mountain experience. From the treeless slopes off Trailridge Road, to the mountain goats and elk that wander in full view of the passing traffic, to pristine lakes nestled in Alpine valleys, the park preserves a chunk of the state's heritage. Any visit to Estes Park would not be complete without a trip into the park for a picnic or short hike.

But Estes Park ranks as a destination itself. A main street lined with shops and restaurants draws day-trippers from cities along the Front Range. People can combine a shopping trip with a bike rental from a local shop, and get a little exercise after lunch. For a longer stay, hotels and camping (inside and outside the park) abound. Have you considered pampering yourself at the Stanley Hotel, the inspiration for Stephen King's *The Shining*?

TRAIL: *Fraser River / Winter Park*
DISTANCE: *4.9 miles*
SURFACE: *paved*
DIFFICULTY: *easy*

Grand County has been referred to as "Denver's playground". Thousands of urban dwellers regularly come up weekly to ski at Winter Park, the ski area owned by Denver. Hordes of people arrive every summer weekend to play on Lake Granby or visit Rocky Mountain National Park.

With the area's emphasis on recreation, you'd have to guess the bicycling excels here. It does. Mountain bike rides for all skills beckon near the ski resort and in the national forest. A fine paved trail runs from the resort to Fraser. And the county has one of the state's most far-reaching master plans for trail development . When built out, they will have a recreation trail running from Berthoud Pass to Rabbit Ears Pass, with a spur to Grand Lake and the national park. All told, the plan calls for roughly one hundred miles of off-street trails.

The current trail lies in the upper reaches of the Fraser River Valley. Leaving from the ski area, it runs along the river through national forest land. Whether the land is wooded or the pastures offer views of the surrounding peaks, the scenery provides for a memorable ride.

The 'high' end of the trail starts in the resort, on Trademark Dr near Winter Park Dr. Turn left onto the trail and quickly enter the woods. Nature surrounds you on this opening stretch as you follow the winding stream downhill. Chances are good for seeing fishermen in the river!

Benches and tables along the trail encourage you to take your time, maybe enjoy a picnic lunch. Despite the fact that the trail runs slightly downhill, be sure to watch your speed, as the trail does have sharp curves.

You soon pass a small trailhead located on US40 (0.8 miles), followed by a short tunnel under the highway. On the

other side you continue through the woods. Pedestrian traffic in the campground (1.2-1.4) may share the trail with you, but otherwise enjoy the solitude – it doesn't last. By mile 1.6 the path runs just below the highway, with the traffic out of sight but not out of sound.

It doesn't take long to enter the town (1.9), where the trail runs alongside the road. The Visitor's Center marks the unofficial center of town (2.4), and also offers another convenient trailhead. It also offers the only stoplight in town, making this the best place to cross the busy highway.

On the other side, follow the trail out of town (3.1). Now a thin row of trees separate you from the highway, providing a minimal buffer. They end quickly as the trail veers from the road (3.4), entering a wide grassy valley. Views here spread to the mountains bordering both sides of the valley.

The trail rolls through the meadow, returning close to US40 before reaching Fraser (4.6). It now runs in front of the Fraser Valley Center, finally ending at the traffic light (4.9). But not for long! Work on the next section of trail, from Fraser to Granby, is currently underway. This extension will add better than another dozen miles to the ride.

What's up? The priorities have not yet been set. Either the trail will continue down valley to Grand Lake, or it will creep uphill toward Berthoud Pass. In either case, the trail will continue to be a showcase for the growth of biking in the state.

WHAT ELSE:

Winter Park's summer attractions now compete with its ski image. All the standard outdoor activities are offered. An hour to the north lies the town and lake of Grand Lake. This, the largest natural body of water in Colorado, offers boating and fishing in a quaint setting. Check out the two-story miniature golf-course in town! Grand Lake also forms the western gateway into Rocky Mountain National Park.

In the resort itself, outdoor music attracts throngs of tourists in July. On two separate weekends, the American Music and the Winter Park Jazz Festivals delight the crowds.

Lodging is readily available in the resort. Restaurants offer food for all price levels, and nightlife abounds. Bicycle rentals and repairs can be had in outlets throughout the town.

TRAIL:	*Clear Creek / Idaho Springs to Georgetown*
DISTANCE:	*3.3 (path) + 14.2 (street) miles*
SURFACE:	*paved*
DIFFICULTY:	*moderate to strenuous -- light traffic on roads*

Clear Creek Canyon: for many, it exists only to allow them to reach their mountain playgrounds (and to slow their return home with traffic bottlenecks through Idaho Springs). Early miners struggled with travel through it, trying to trahsport their precious metals to market. The railroads made it to Georgetown in 1877 with little difficulty, but it took seven more years to penetrate two miles further to Silver Plume. Today it hosts a pivotal link of a hoped-for bike trail stretching east-to-west across the state.

Georgetown, located off I-70 one exit north of US40, is a popular stopping point for tourists and travelers. Families who settled the town had generally higher morals than the saloon-and-brothel crowd in most gold camps, and built many fine Victorian mansions and buildings. Their esteemed volunteer fire department kept the town from burning down (as many towns did), resulting in over 200 original buildings still standing today. Also still standing (though no longer using the original tracks) is the Georgetown Loop Railroad, the "railroader's nightmare" that climbed to Silver Plume. The train runs the three-mile route daily every summer, taking riders on an hour-long trip back in history.

The bike route detailed here is the book's only ride that is mostly on regular streets. After leaving the trail in Idaho Springs, it follows the old US6 up canyon to Georgetown. Though open to traffic, most cars instead speed by I-70, leaving this lightly traveled. The exception is on summer Sundays, when autos attempting to bypass the freeway backups clog the old road. I can't recommend this route on those days; Saturdays, though, often see groups of bicyclists here.

You can access this route south of Idaho Springs. The

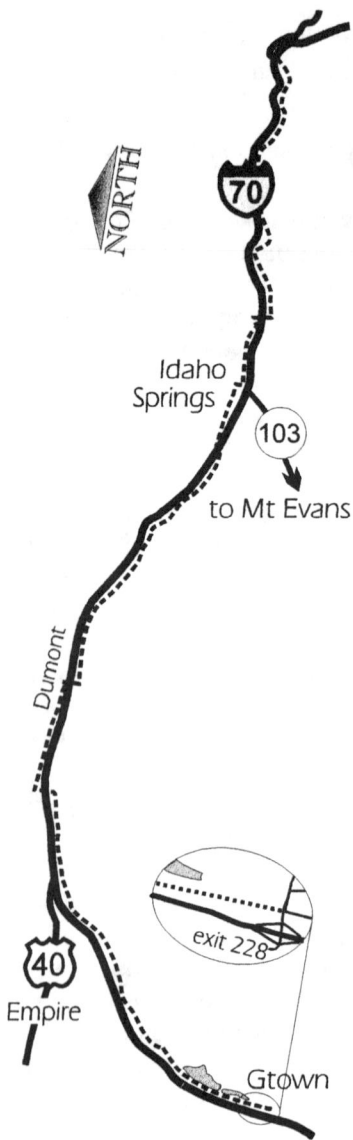

NORTH

70

Idaho
Springs

103

to Mt Evans

Dumont

exit 228

40

Empire

Gtown

US6/Clear Creek Canyon exit (exit 244) off I-70 brings you to a dirt parking area in the shade of the freeway curve. Cross over the creek and under the interstate to find the trail on the old highway 6. Ignore the dead end signs and pylons – they mean to keep out cars.

The path soon narrows as it passes through the trees by the creek. Traffic noise from I-70 across the creek ruins the illusion of solitude, but you can smell the fresh, pine-scented air. The trail climbs up and down a few short hills, but watch your speed. Sand and stones sometimes fill the path, and the author was once surprised by a car that had snuck through the barriers.

Head straight on the old road after the stop sign at the Hidden Valley junction (1.5 miles). Laugh at the traffic across the creek as you follow the stream around bends, and cross the creek (2.3) when I-70 enters the twin tunnels. The old road ends here, so cross Clear Creek again on the wooden bridge (2.5). Turn right on the road, then left on the path at the top of the rise (2.6). If the road has turned to gravel, you've

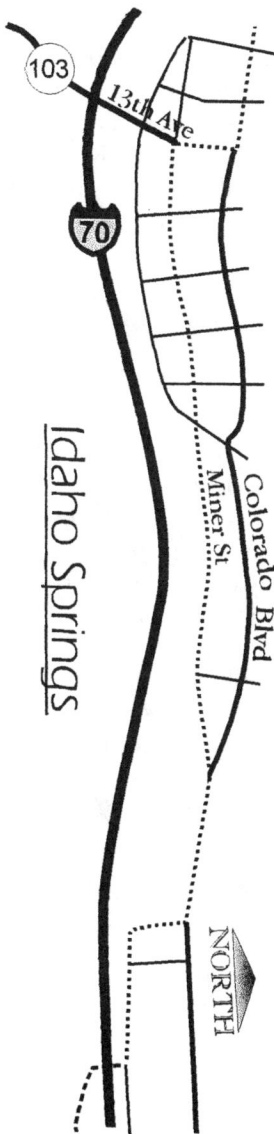

gone just too far!

Pass the house and the cement block to regain the trail, heading into the trees. Enjoy the isolation from I-70; it doesn't last long! The trail dumps back on the side road (now paved) at mile 3.1, and follows it to the Idaho Springs junction (3.5). Don't turn here, but head toward the ballfields. The trail starts again behind the fields (3.7), and climbs to a crest (4.0) before dropping to a tunnel under I-70 (4.1). Again, watch for sand here.

Now we're on streets for the rest of the ride. Turn left in the alley, right on 25th Ave, and left on Colorado Blvd. After passing Safeway, bear left when the road splits (by the statue of Steve Canyon) to ride into 'downtown'. Turn right on 13th (5.2) at downtown's edge, and left back onto Colorado to head out of town. Some of the houses on your way west are worth noting.

Don't miss the left turn onto Stanley Rd (6.0). This takes you back across Clear Creek on the old highway, passing old mining buildings. Stay on County Rd 312 as it follows the creek until mile 10.1, when you turn right to cross I-70 and enter Dumont. Hang an immediate left onto County Rd 308, and parallel the freeway into Downiesville (10.9). A ski rental shop and Burger King anchor this exit off I-70. Keep going straight, passing under the interstate (11.7) and over the creek

(12.1) onto County Rd 306. Don't go under the freeway here!

As you skirt the I-70/US40 interchange, the road encounters its biggest hill of the ride (13.5). Downshift and you'll find it over quickly (13.9), and the road levels off again. Go straight at the stop sign for the bridge, and 306 will turn into Alvarado Rd. Houses dot the road as the canyon widens, and you may meet a couple of cars. One last climb brings you to the reservoir (16.1), and you reach the outskirts of town at mile 17.5. Congratulations! You've just climbed over 1200'. They must have put that ice cream shop on the corner to help you celebrate!

WHAT ELSE:

This area ranks more as a travel corridor than a destination resort. Many of the area attractions relate to its mining history, with mine tours and museums in or around both towns. The Georgetown Loop Railroad draws the most visitors, with its historic three-mile stretch of track that loops back and passes over itself. Georgetown also offers a historic district jammed with shops and restaurants.

Food and lodging is available throughout the canyon, though the selection is less than in the major resorts over Loveland or Berthoud Pass. For bike rentals, you can stop in Idaho Springs to pick up wheels for the day.

TRAIL: *Woodland Park to Manitou Lake*
DISTANCE: *7.1 miles*
SURFACE: *paved*
DIFFICULTY: *easy to moderate*

In the hills west of Colorado Springs, major trail projects are underway or planned. Visions of an off-street path running from Woodland Park to the plains are slowly turning into reality. A general course for the trail – known as the Ute Pass Trail Corridor – has been defined, and small segments are in place. When complete, this trail (along with several in the Colorado Springs area) will comprise an important part of the American Discovery Trail.

The ADT is a proposed coast-to-coast recreational trail cutting through the heart of the country. Proposed in 1989 by *Backpacker* magazine and the American Hiking Society, it aims to link cities, countryside, national parks and more in a path for hikers, bikers, and equestrians. A general route currently exists, but development of actual trails (and redirection of the trail) continues on a state-by-state basis.

The longest existing trail currently in the Ute Pass Trail Corridor begins in Woodland Park. Running 7.1 miles from town to Manitou Lake, it passes through the pines and scrub oak of the national forest. The surrounding hills add to the beauty of the trail.

The trail currently starts at CO67 and County Rd, ½ mile north of US24. Unfortunately, there is no trailhead here or elsewhere in town. Officials have plans to extend the trail to US24, with a trailhead at Midland Ave, but it has not happened as of early 1999.

The trail closely follows CO67 as it heads north. It crosses many side streets as it works its way out of town, past houses and small businesses. Trees provide shade as the trail enters the national forest, running by campgrounds on the way to the lake. It does pass one parking/picnic area on the east side of the

63

Manitou
Lake Park

NORTH

67

Kelley Rd

County Rd

24

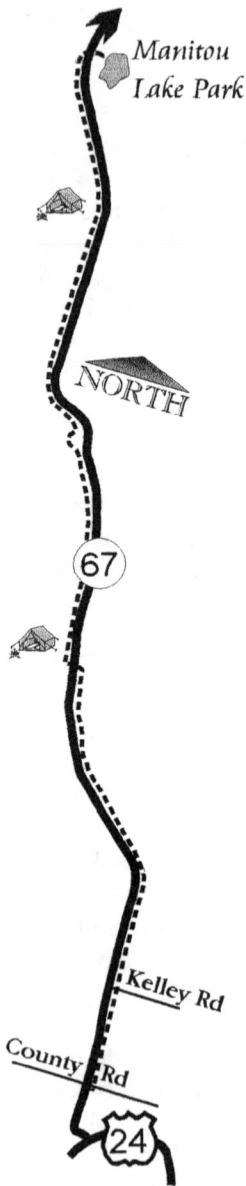

road, shortly before tunneling under the highway and running in and out of view on the road's west side.

The trail ends at Manitou Lake, which charges a small fee for parking and day use. You may wish to stop here and enjoy the grounds before heading back to town.

WHAT ELSE:

Woodland Park is more of a way station than a final destination. Cripple Creek, the historic mining town, lies 25 miles south of here, offering gambling and beautiful countryside. Fifteen miles to the west, Florissant Fossil Beds National Monument illustrates what life was like in this region eons ago. Want to see petrified tree stumps? This is the place to go.

The town of Woodland Park is large enough to offer lodging and restaurants, but don't expect resort-level options. Camping is available at Manitou Lake. If you hope to bicycle here, you'd best bring your own equipment.

NORTH FRONT RANGE

'Growth' is the word in northern Colorado. The state's economy and well-educated populace (due in part to the universities in Boulder, Fort Collins, and Greeley) has attracted scores of high-tech companies. The resulting boom has resulted in much building throughout the area.

The residents have also demanded outlets for recreation, and governments have responded. Several multi-use trails follow the waterways draining the region, and new developments often add paths through the required green space. In the next several years, many of those trails will grow together, providing a network running town-to-town. The Cache la Poudre Trail is leading the way: plans have it complete from Greeley to the Larimer County line by 2001.

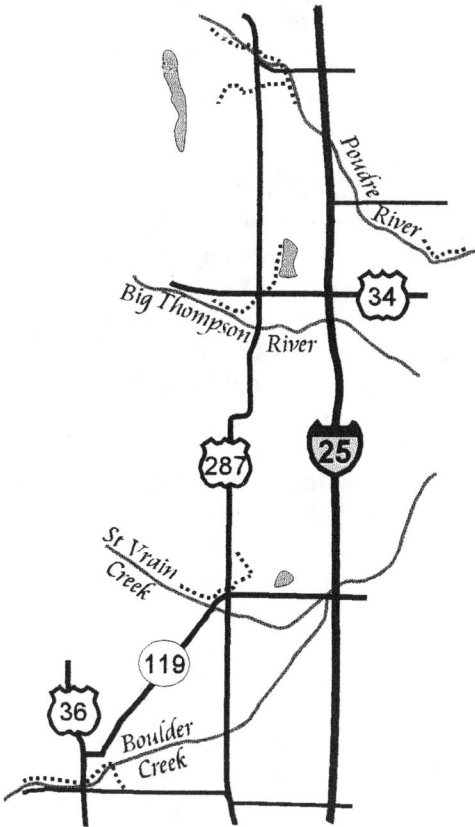

TRAIL: *Cache la Poudre River / Fort Collins*
DISTANCE: *8.4 miles*
SURFACE: *paved, concrete*
DIFFICULTY: *easy*

In the fall of 1836, French fur traders passed through this area en route to a Rendezvous on the Green River. They camped for the night on the banks of a gentle river, and woke in the morning mired in the deep snow of an early season storm. The wagon train remained stuck for a week, forcing them to lighten their load. They dug a large pit, lined it with pine boughs and animal skins, and buried any supplies not essential to their journey – which included several hundred pounds of gunpowder. They called this spot along the river *Cache la Poudre*, 'the hiding place of the powder'.

Nowadays, bikers have replaced fur traders along the Cache la Poudre River. From the western edge of the city, beside the old downtown, and past high-tech companies fueling the town's growth, the river ties the city together.

The western terminus of the bike trail lies on Taft Hill Rd, 1.5 miles north of LaPorte Ave. Parking is available at the trailhead. For the first 0.5 miles gravel mounds and pits surround the trail, but the river comes into view after you pass through a small tunnel. Soon the gravel operations succumb to fields and farms, with great views of the foothills behind you (to appreciate on the return trip). The trail dips under Shields St at 1.1 miles, and (with the exception of one junky area) the river looks fairly wild.

After passing a bridge to walking trails (1.6) and the bridge to the Hickory St Trail (2.0), you enter Lee Martinez Park. This wide, groomed open space attracts many visitors, and lasts until mile 2.3. The trail then passes under College Ave (US287) (2.4) and railroad tracks (2.5) as it passes the edge of downtown. Not that you'll see skyscrapers here – it's a mix of low buildings (both new and old) and open fields. That mix continues as the

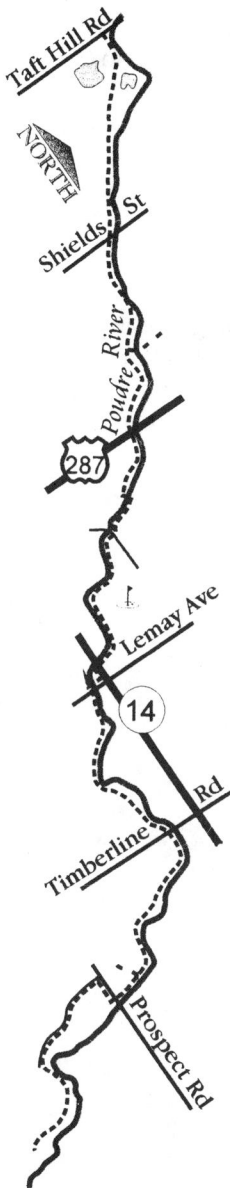

trail joins Linden St (2.8) to cross over the
river, then cuts under Lincoln Ave (3.1).

At mile 3.4, the trail skirts a golf course
on the left. A small trailhead (parking only)
follows off Lemay Ave at Mulberry St
(CO14) (4.0), then the trail dives under
Mulberry. On the opposite side it joins the
sidewalk on Lemay to again cross the
river, then curls back to cross under the
street (4.4). You now find yourself in a
wetland area – thick stands of trees, with
birds chattering as you pass by. The rural
feeling takes over as you see highway 14
fall away to the north.

Another street (Timberline Rd) passes
overhead at mile 5.9, followed by land
scraped clean – getting ready for more
high-tech companies? Who knows? Soon
you are back in the bottomlands, alone
with the river and trees. The Spring Creek
Trail branches to the right at mile 6.6; stay
left to finish this ride.

After ducking under Prospect Rd (6.8),
the trail joins the sidewalk and takes a left
on Sharp Point Drive. For a short time you
travel between ponds reclaimed from
gravel pits and a smattering of technology
firms. About now your nose should
announce the presence of the Drake
Waste Water Reclamation Plant, next to
the Prospect Points trailhead (7.8). Would
you really want to fish here? Thankfully
the, er, aroma passes quickly.

At mile 8.1 take the wooden bridge
over the ditch, and bear left into the
Environmental Learning Center. Across the

river, hiking trails beckon – but no bikes allowed! At trails end (8.4), a plain wooden building houses the Raptor Rehab Center. Be sure to wander over and check out the eagles, hawks and owls recovering from various injuries.

Current plans are to extend the trail further down river. By 2002 or 2003, hopes are to make it under I-25 to Timnath.

WHAT ELSE:

Fort Collins is a college town, which means lots of inexpensive and ethnic food, and lots of lodging. Some of the major recreational draws are Horsetooth Reservoir for boating and fishing, and Poudre Canyon for whitewater rafting and fishing. Mountain biking is big here, and stores in town rent equipment.

TRAIL: *Spring Creek / Fort Collins*
DISTANCE: *5.5 miles*
SURFACE: *paved*
DIFFICULTY: *easy*

On Monday, July 28th, 1997, Ft. Collins residents were preparing for bed, remarking on the wet days that finally ended a hot and dry summer. Since Sunday afternoon, ten to fourteen inches had fallen – at rates up to six inches per hour. When the excessive water (two to three times the amount predicted for a 500-year storm) finally overflowed the creek system, a wall of water came rushing down Spring Creek. Two trailer parks were wiped out, five people died, and over $100 million in damages were logged.

Since then the city has restored the greenway along the creek (without the trailer parks). Today a bike ride along the tame creek gives no indication of the damage it caused. Spring Creek is again a gentle stream winding through city parks and quiet neighborhoods.

Starting at the Poudre River Trail north of Prospect Rd, the trail heads west between business parks and open space ponds. After crossing under Prospect (0.5 miles), you can glimpse the creek for the first time, winding through the reeds. Timberline Rd quickly passes overhead (0.7), and the trail climbs to street level to cross railroad tracks.

Follow the trail away from the road (0.8) past a Prairie Management Area into more open space. A red dirt trail for running begins immediately to your side, and accompanies the trail off and on. At mile 1.0 you pass well under a railroad trestle, then under Riverside Ave (1.1) into Edora Park. Across the creek lies tennis courts, and a mountain bike course sits to your right. Look here also for the first of the signs showing the water level during the flood.

Leave Edora Park behind (1.6) for a ride through a wild strip hemmed in by condos and businesses. A rural feel returnsafter

Drake Rd

NORTH

Shields St

287

Stuart St

Lemay Ave

Timberline Rd

Prospect Rd

Poudre River

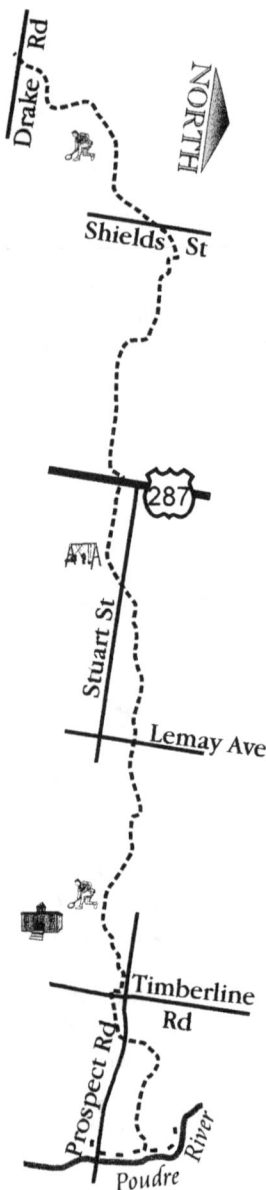

passing under Lemay Ave (1.9), with horse properties and farm equipment visible. After crisscrossing the creek, you briefly join Alpert Ct (2.5) before diving under Stover St and Stuart St (2.7). Spring Park now lies directly ahead (2.8), with a pond, parking, and restroom facilities.

The trail crosses under College Ave at mile 3.1, dropping you into the area where the trailer parks once sat. Now it's a grassy park dotted with trees. Take a gander at the water level sign here, far above your head, to get a feel for how much water rushed through after breaching the railroad.

Cross under the railroad tracks at mile 3.2, then head left on the frontage road until regaining the trail on the right (3.3). You circle a large open space owned by CSU as you follow an irrigation canal back to the creek. Now the creek bed is wide with low dams as you pass between houses on your way west. Cross over the creek (4.2), and take the path's left fork (the right heads into the neighborhood). At 4.4 miles you cross under Shields St, the trail's last major tunnel.

Quickly you enter Rolland Moore Park (4.6), a huge park complex with two open space areas attached. The first side trail branches off into Fisher Natural Area (4.8), eleven acres with cottonwood trees and a bicycle motocross course. Stay left instead to pass the tennis and volleyball courts. Next up is a spur into Ross Natural Area (5.1), thirty acres of grasslands, wetlands, and wildlife viewing. The main trail stays right, ducking under Drake Road before ending at mile 5.5.

Another short (0.7 mile) stretch of trail exists west of Taft Hill Rd. The city currently plans to link that stretch with the main trail by 2001, providing a link with the Foothills Trail.

WHAT ELSE:

See the previous writeup.

TRAIL: *Cache la Poudre River / Windsor*
DISTANCE: *3.0 miles in early 1999*
SURFACE: *concrete*
DIFFICULTY: *easy*

Windsor is a fine example of the towns that make up the 'real' Colorado. Never a major draw for tourists, it retains a small-town feeling often lost in its big neighbors of Fort Collins, Loveland, and Greeley. As with most plains towns, agriculture and ranching dominated its early economy. The Kodak plant outside town now provides many well-paying jobs, and the northern Colorado 'techno-business boom' has spurred additional growth.

Windsor has also focused on recreation. It occupies a spot along the Poudre River halfway between Fort Collins and Greeley. Eventually a bikeway along the river will connect the two college towns, running forty miles through open plains and river bottomland. Windsor will occupy the center of that line, providing supplies and a rest haven for long-distance cyclists.

The longest stretch of the Poudre Trail in Weld County is located southeast of the town, behind the Kodak plant. Built by Kodak, the trail begins at CO257 on the north side of the river. It closely follows the meandering waterway, at times running through the trees of the bottomland, other times edging along the irrigated farmland. Birds call to you from the leafy trees, protesting your invasion.

Though a Kodak project, they jointly manage the trail with the city of Windsor and Weld County. It runs for 3.0 miles, concrete for its whole length (except, as of early 1999, for one dirt gap of one hundred yards). On the trail's eastern edge, it ends abruptly at a bridge over the stream. You can see the signs of trail building on the opposite bank.

And they are quickly building more trail! In early 1999 Greeley's Montfort family donated $250,000 to extend the trail. A pending GOCO grant provides more money for connecting

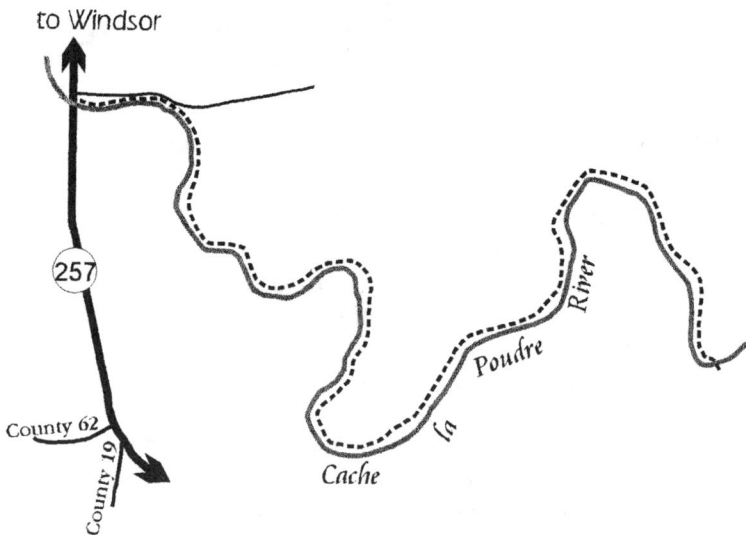

to Windsor

257

County 62

County 19

Cache la Poudre River

links. In summer 1999, officials expect to open three more miles on the east of the present trail, and hope to link a one-mile stretch in the Water Valley subdivision and a half-mile leg in Eastman Park to the main trail. In addition, an off-street bike path now runs two miles alongside Eastman Park Rd, providing access to the Kodak plant for bicycle commuters.

If all goes as planned, the bikeway will run for nine miles south and east of Windsor by the end of 1999. Longer-term plans call for completing the bikeway between Greeley and the Larimer County line by 2001, depending on negotiations with land owners.

WHAT ELSE:

Windsor is a smaller town. It does offer restaurants and lodging, and more services are available in the nearby towns of Greeley and Fort Collins.

TRAIL: *Big Thompson River to Boyd Lake / Loveland*
DISTANCE: *7.9 (path) + 0.8 (street) miles*
SURFACE: *paved, concrete*
DIFFICULTY: *easy, except for connection to fairgrounds*

Loveland's history has always been tied to transportation. In 1862 a predecessor settlement named St. Louis became part of the Overland Stage Line. When the railroad came through in the 1870s, people platted a new town near the tracks and named it after the railroad president, W. A. H. Loveland.

It still occupies a strategic position at the mouth of the Big Thompson canyon. US34 crosses town east-to-west, then navigates the canyon to deliver tourists to Rocky Mountain National Park. US287 splits the town on a north/south axis, connecting it to Fort Collins and to the Denver metro area.

Loveland also has a well-developed bike path. The master plan calls for a loop trail encircling much of the town and surrounding countryside. The current path, roughly half of that goal, follows a 'J' shaped-route to tie the heart of the city to nearby Boyd Lake State Park. This park boasts over 1,700 surface-acres of water for fishing, boating, and sailing. A sandy beach and seasonally warm water make Boyd a favorite spot for windsurfers, water-skiers and swimmers.

The northern terminus of the trail lies near the north end of the lake. From the parking and picnic area at the end of the park road, it starts by closely following the shoreline. After crossing the park road (1.2 miles), it temporarily veers away from the lake. Soon it recrosses the road, merging with the trail in the popular beach area (1.8). Mind your speed among the crowds on the beach.

When the trail splits, follow the left fork along the shore. Slowly the trail swings to the west, finally crossing a lake outlet at mile 2.7. As it turns due south, you pedal by Heinricy Lake to the right. Soon you find yourself in Seven Lakes Park (3.1), a city park with trails looping through it. Stay to the left to cross the

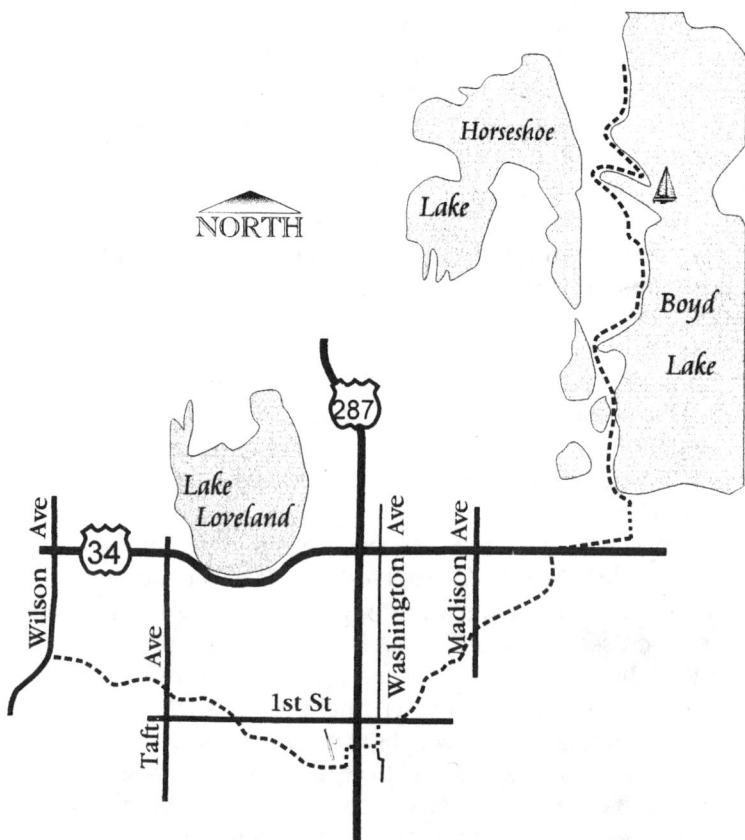

park.

    Leave the park (3.8) by crossing 18th St onto Denver Ave. Follow this side road until the trail cuts to the right (4.0), following the canal under Eisenhower Blvd/US34 (4.2). On the opposite side, the trail follows the canal through an open field bordered by industry on the right.

    The trail crosses Madison Ave at mile 5.0, then has its own stoplight controlling bike traffic over the railroad tracks. You now pedal through a residential district, following the canal between back yards and across several side streets. Watch for the emu in one of the first yards you pass! Once you reach the Civic Center (5.6), the trail curves again to parallel 1st St (5.8).

Bike route signs tell you to cross 1st at Washington Ave (6.0) Now on city streets, you take Washington to the next street, and turn right on 3rd St SE (6.1). This quickly takes you to Lincoln Ave, where things get dicey.

In downtown Loveland, US287 is split onto separate north- and south-bound streets. Lincoln carries the north-bound traffic, but we need to head south on the trail. When traffic is clear, jog south several yards on Lincoln and quickly turn right into the continuation of 3rd St SE. (You will see the bike signs once you turn.) The next cross-street is Cleveland (6.4), carrying south-bound 287 traffic. Follow that south to the park on 5th St SE (6.5). NOTE: on your return, follow 5th to Lincoln and take that north to 3rd.

Once in the park, the trail begins again (6.6), and immediately branches. The left fork winds by the Larimer County Fairgrounds, then turns east along the Big Thompson River. It crosses under US287 (7.4), but no ramps provide access to the highway. This spur enters a wild area before quickly hitting a dead-end (7.5). If you're lucky you may glimpse wildlife here – I saw a deer trotting right at me when I scouted the trail.

Soon this spur will extend to replace the above-described tangle with US287. An extension to 8th St SE was being staked at this book's press time, and should be completed before summer 1999. Completion of the path to 4th St SE and Washington (where the route would run a short distance on city streets) is expected in the fall.

The main trail continues straight ahead from the fork. It crosses over the Big Thompson, then under the railroad tracks (6.7). To the left are reclaimed gravel ponds, to the right a river that looks more like an irrigation ditch. After passing under 1st St (7.4), you enter Centennial Park, though little of the park is visible from the trail.

As you proceed west, the terrain gradually grows wilder.

After diving under Taft Ave (7.9) the river once again resembles a river, with gravel bars and stands of trees. The open space surrounding the river becomes wide, and houses no longer crowd the trail. The trail feels as remote as it gets inside the city. A side trail at mile 8.3 runs 0.3 miles into a nearby neighborhood, crossing Dotsero and Bushnell Streets in the process. The main path follows the river, ending at Wilson Ave (8.7).

WHAT ELSE:

Loveland's most noted annual event is early August's Sculpture in the Park. Two hundred sculptors come to Benson Park each year to sell and display their work for thousands of visitors. Creations can be had for as little as $400, or you can drop $60,000 on the perfect piece for your dining room.

The town is large enough to offer a large selection of hotels, motels, and restaurants.

TRAIL: *St. Vrain Creek & Rough'n'Ready Ditch / Longmont*
DISTANCE: *6.3 (path) + 1.8 (street) miles*
SURFACE: *paved, concrete*
DIFFICULTY: *easy – moderate traffic on city streets*

Longmont got an early start on its bike path network. In the mid-70s the city opened the first stretch of the St. Vrain Greenway, a 1/3 mile path along the creek from Main St to Pratt Parkway. After a little work in the early 80s, the city developed a master plan in 1992. Trail building inside the master plan soon accelerated, and more trails are still to come.

While no trail runs through the whole city, well-marked bike lanes on city streets help to connect the various pieces. The three longest trails can be connected with a quiet ride through the heart of downtown, giving a sampling of the variety the town has to offer.

This ride is broken into three sections. The first, and by far the most pleasant, runs along the St. Vrain River. The western trailhead is currently at Golden Ponds, on 3rd Ave Pl west of Hover. This nature area, named after V. V. Golden who mined gravel here, has 1.5 miles of dirt trails around the ponds. Catch and release fishing is popular here, and picnic tables abound. From the end of the parking area, head west on the concrete trail and follow it between ponds and over the river (0.3 miles).

The river retains a wild feel throughout the length of the ride. Trees line its banks, and the stream flows around gravel deposits. After crossing under Hover Rd (0.9) into Fairground Park, crushed gravel trails (for hiking only) head into the river's woods. Other trails wander through gardens or around Fairground Lake.

At 1.3 miles the path forks. The right branch curves around the lake; take the left branch over the river. Now the wild strip bordering the river narrows as it heads toward the heart of the city. Businesses are never far to the side as the trail crosses under Sunset St (1.6), Boston Ave (1.9), and the railroad

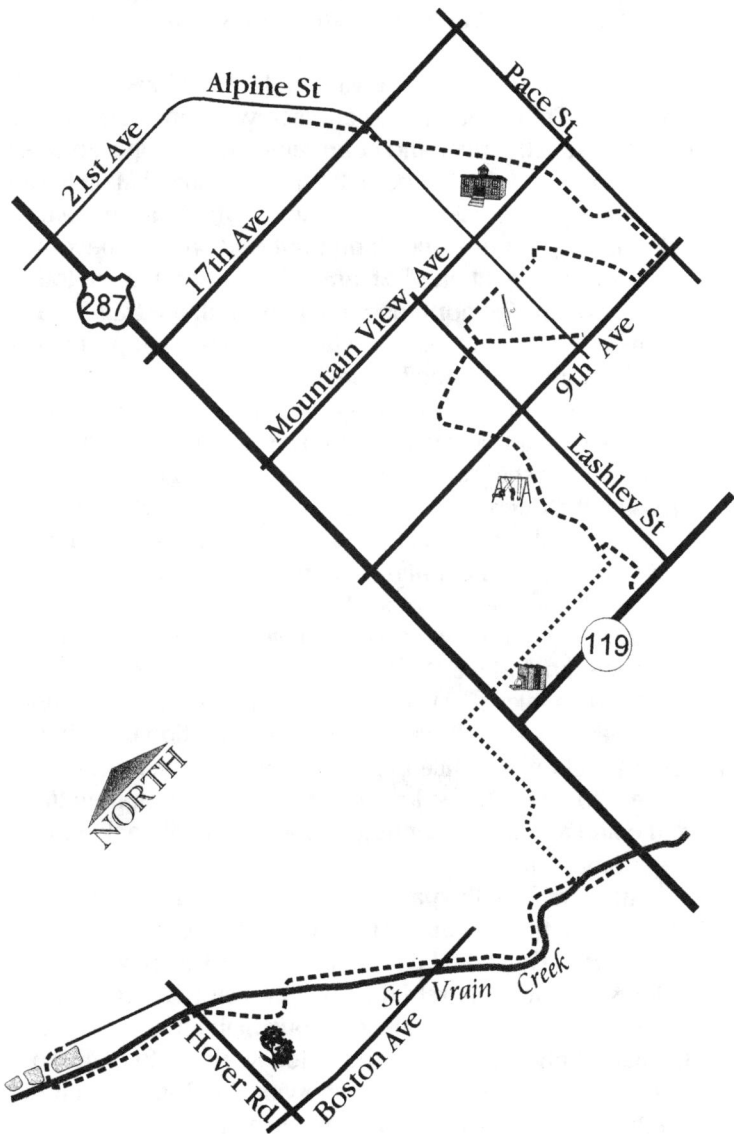

(2.2). Still the trail keeps a relaxing feel, staying close above the waterway.

This stretch ends after diving under Pratt Pkwy (2.6). The Greenway Trail continues by corkscrewing up to street level then crossing the river and continuing on the opposite side. However, it ends in another 0.3 miles just shy of Main St (an extension is in the works). To connect with trails to the east, skip that leg and head north on Pratt (which soon becomes Terry St). Turn right on 4th St, and take that east to the trail at Kensington St. Jog north one block to catch the trail. Total distance for this route is 1.5 miles, and takes you past old house, through downtown, and by the library.

The path through Kensington Park actually starts a few blocks south at Rothrock Pl. From a parking area between Martin and Lashely Sts, it heads north along a concrete canal, crossing the ditch (0.2) at 5th and Kensington (where you will connect). A short block later it re-crosses it, entering the widest part of the park. The trail hops across Longs Peak Ave (0.7) before leaving the park at 9th Ave (0.9).

Here the ditch reverts to native vegetation as it continues north into an undeveloped lot. It soon curves, crossing Martin (1.1) and Lashley (1.3) and entering Clark Centennial Park. However, this stretch was under reconstruction in spring 1999 and may change. While this work is underway, an alternate route is to follow the sidewalk on 9th to Alpine St, then turn left and catch a trail along another concrete canal back into Clark Centennial Park.

After entering the park, cross the concrete canal and work your way to the parking lot in the northeast corner. Cross Alpine onto Crystal Ct, and take it to the end (1.9). A rough asphalt trail follows another concrete drainage between houses, ending at 9th (2.3). Take the sidewalk left along high fences, crossing Granite Ct and curving around to follow Pace Rd (2.4). Soon the trail breaks away from Pace, following the Rough and Ready Ditch. Now houses only clutter the view to the left; to the right you can see some of the (rapidly disappearing) farmland east of town.

At 3.0 miles the trail crosses Mountain View Ave, becoming smooth concrete again. It glides by Skyline High and then more houses. Watch the big trees scattered along the ditch – you may see a treehouse or two! When the trail reaches Alpine St (3.6) the ditch temporarily disappears. Turn right on Alpine to cross 17th Ave, and catch the trail (and ditch) again at Sunlight Dr (3.7). It continues rambling northwest until finally ending at 21st Ave (4.3). You can return along the same path, or take Lashley or Alpine back to Clark Centennial Park to cut off a little distance.

WHAT ELSE:

Lodging is readily available in the town, and restaurants offer food for all price levels. Several bicycle shops can be found through the town; some may offer rentals or demos.

TRAIL:	*Boulder Creek / Boulder*
DISTANCE:	*8.0 miles*
SURFACE:	*concrete, paved, dirt*
DIFFICULTY:	*easy, moderate in canyon*

Boulder is an ideal town for bicycling. Trails weave throughout the city, running both north-to-south and east-to-west. Bike shops abound, and health-conscious residents go out in most any weather. Of all the trails they use, perhaps the most popular is the Boulder Creek Trail.

The eastern end of the trail is the easiest to reach. Starting at Arapahoe Rd just west of Cherryvale Rd, the trail heads north along South Boulder Creek. The wooded terrain provides a quick escape from the feel of the city. After passing under the railroad tracks, the trail forks (0.5), with the right branch crossing the creek and ending at the Stazio ballfields. The main track continues ahead, with businesses to your left and (eventually) a pond on your right.

At the far edge of the pond the trail again forks (1.1). The right branch follows Boulder Creek 0.3 miles, ending at Valmont Rd. For this ride, take the left branch upstream. It quickly passes under 55th St, then runs along another pond in the open space bordering Pearl St. Take the left branch again when the path splits at mile 1.9; the straight-ahead route continues along Pearl. The main path keeps open space to the left as it returns to the creek, crossing under the railroad tracks again as it works it way west. The forested area surrounding the creek has many side paths for walkers and joggers; some workers from the area companies may find an unused log for an impromptu picnic.

The trail briefly joins the Foothills Parkway Trail at 2.4 miles; to the right it runs back to Pearl St and beyond. Follow it to the left as it crosses the creek, then hang right at mile 2.5 as the Foothills Parkway Trail continues south. Our trail immediately dives under Foothills Pkwy then continues belowstreet level, crossing under Arapahoe at mile 2.8. Now the land to the south

119

NORTH

Broadway

Folsom St

36

157

Pearl Pkwy

Arapahoe Ave

55th St

is open, part of the CU athletic complex. The Skunk Creek Trail to your left leads into this area, but bear right instead. A greenhouse signals the end of open space, and soon you're pedaling behind residences.

After crossing under 30th St (3.3) and over the creek, Scott Carpenter Park sits on your right. This park is popular year-round, for the sledding hill in the winter and the swimming pool in the summer. (A right fork at the park's edge connects with the Crossroads Shopping Center.) Past the park, the trail again has houses and businesses to one side. However, the creek always stays semi-wild, with large trees providing shade on hot days. Cross under 28th St at mile 3.6, and watch out for foot traffic from the Harvest House and the people enjoying the tennis and volleyball courts by the trailside. Continue west, passing under Folsom St at mile 3.9.

Now bluffs rise steeply across the creek, and university buildings perch atop the hill. The trail passes by nice homes beneath the bluff as it heads west. At one point it splits into two one-way lanes as it passes a day-care area. It jogs sharply to cross under 17th St (4.4), emerging behind Boulder High School. After passing the football field, you pass under Arapahoe again (4.8). On the adjacent street, a farmer's market peddles fresh produce during the summer.

After passing the bandshell, the trail slides under Broadway (4.9) to the library park complex, one of the busiest stretches of the trail. Two bridges cross the creek to access Boulder Public Library as the path continues straight; in late spring you're likely to see inner tubers playing in the cold waters. The path passes under 9th St at mile 5.1 and circles around Kid's Pond, where the tykes fish. Again, several dirt side paths let walkers and joggers escape into the trees. At 5.3 miles you cross under 6th St and pass by the Justice Center – on the far side you may want to stop and wander through the xeriscape garden planted there.

A bridge at mile 5.8 dumps you into Eben G. Fine Park, at the gateway to Boulder Canyon. (Restrooms are unlocked here in season.) As the trail follows the creek into the canyon, it passes a kayak course – during runoff season you can watch athletes practice their strokes. The trail now begins to climb, not steeply but consistently. It crosses a private driveway at mile 6.2, then passes under CO119 (6.7).

As the trail exits the tunnel, it turns to gravel. Though the surface is still well-graded, it is not recommended for road (skinny-tire) bikes. After passing a cliff popular with rock climbers, it crosses the creek and heads further up canyon. Another bridge at mile 7.7 recrosses the creek, and the trail finally ends at mile 8.0.

WHAT ELSE:

This college town lies in the foothills, where outdoor recreation abounds. South of town, Eldorado Springs offers swimming, hiking, or a place to watch world-class rock climbers. One must-see for visitors is the Pearl St Mall, an open-strip for shopping or watching the buskers juggle, play music, contort themselves, translate zip codes to towns, and more. All services are available in town.

SOUTH FRONT RANGE

Though the cities and towns of the southern Front Range may not get as much 'press' as their neighbors to the north, they have just as much to offer. The Air Force Academy, which draws over a million visitors per year, ranks as the state's third most popular attraction. Thousands of people flee to Pueblo Lake State Park each weekend to participate in outdoor activities. Cripple Creek offers gambling to those so inclined, and the Royal Gorge amazes visitors with its deep, narrow chasm.

Recreation is not given short shrift here. For bicyclists, horseback riders, and joggers, paths weave through the area. A backbone trail along Monument and Fountain Creeks runs from Palmer Lake to Fountain with only two interruptions, and those missing links may be filled in 1999. Trail projects in Pueblo and further south help to make this a cycling hotbed.

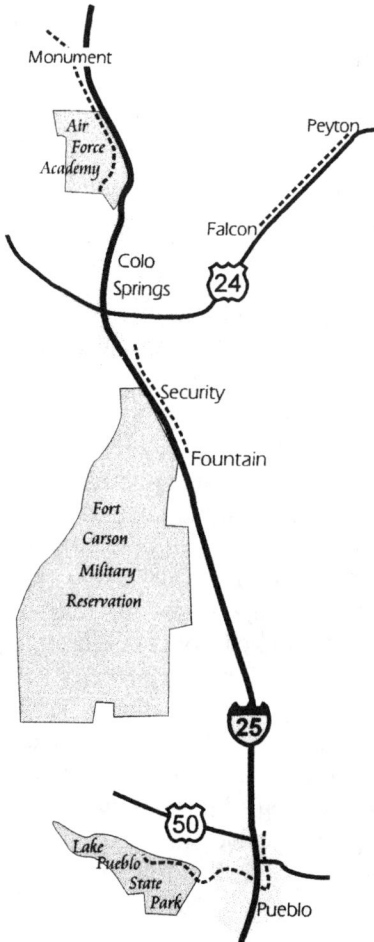

TRAIL: *Monument Creek / Palmer Lake - Air Force Academy*
DISTANCE: *15.3 miles*
SURFACE: *dirt/gravel*
DIFFICULTY: *easy to moderate*

Following World War II, Congress decided that the nation's defense would be well served by having our aviators organized in their own branch of the military. Up to this point, flyers had served under the command of the Army. The new Air Force began operations in July 1947.

Officials quickly realized the need for their own service academy. The Pentagon formed a commission to determine where to locate the school, and they spent years evaluating 580 sites across the country. In the summer of 1954, they announced their choice: the foot of the Rampart Range north of Colorado Springs.

The campus, though largely off limits to tourists, is the third most popular attraction in the state. Most of the one-million-plus annual visitors come to see the 17-spire Cadet Chapel. Others come for golfing, wildlife viewing, hiking, or biking.

A beautiful running/biking trail runs through Academy grounds. With a surface of dirt and sand, it is very popular with joggers. Starting in Palmer Lake, it follows an old rail bed for much of its length. Halfway through the school grounds, though, it heads west to trace a route along Monument Creek.

Since this is a rails-to-trails conversion, it stays level until leaving the rail bed. Trains lacked real hill-climbing power, thus limiting the tracks to 3% grades. The resulting trail provides a gentle ride for most of its length. From a high elevation of 7200' in Palmer Lake, it drops around 60' per mile, dropping to 6400' at the south end of the Academy. Given the hills in and out of the creek's bottomland, you'll actually log a bit more, but the true challenge comes from riding the whole distance.

From the park adjacent to Palmer Lake, the trail takesoff from the restrooms. The early scenery excels, with trees and

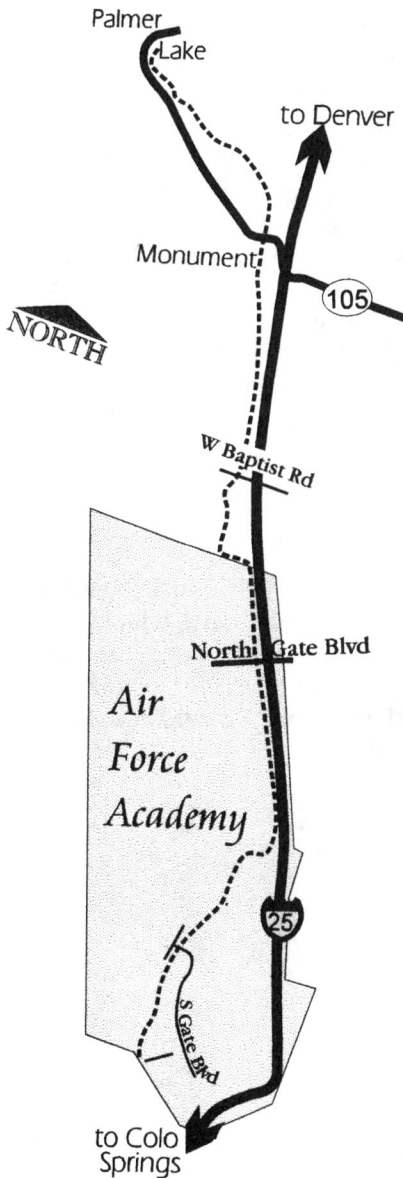

Palmer Lake

to Denver

Monument

NORTH

105

W Baptist Rd

North Gate Blvd

Air
Force
Academy

25

S Gate Blvd

to Colo
Springs

brush backed up by
Elephant Rock and Ben
Lomond Mountain. To the
west the Rampart Range
rises abruptly from the
Monument Valley.

Signs regularly spaced
along the route shed light
on the geology, weather,
wildlife, and history of the
area. Many of the signs are
written with a touch of
whimsy, with such titles as
"My Wild Irish Rose Hips" or
"16" of partly cloudy".

A smattering of houses
announces your arrival in
Monument. In town you will
pass two trailheads with
parking, one on CO105 (3.1
miles) and another on 3rd St
(3.5). After passing the old
Monument Schoolhouse,
the trail leaves town for
more wide-open spaces.

South of Monument the
area takes on a prairie feel.
A wide grassland buffers
you from the traffic on I-25
as the trail parallels the old
road to Denver. After
passing the trailhead on
Baptist Rd (6.2), you leave
the old road behind and
eventually shoot west
toward the freeway and

enter the Academy at mile 7.8. Now the trail runs through scattered trees a short distance from the highway, with a spur leading to the North Gate trailhead at mile 9.1.

The trail leaves the rail bed at mile 11.5, turning sharply and heading into thicker stands of trees along Monument Creek. Now you must navigate a few short, sandy hills that may require walking road bikes as you follow the creek, sometimes above it, sometimes in the bottomlands. The trail passes far below South Gate Blvd (13.7) as the Monument Valley widens and deepens. Trailheads mark the end of the trail at 14.9 and 15.3 miles.

If you prefer to start on the south end, and then cruise downhill on the return ride, you can reach one of the final trailheads by entering the Academy on South Gate Blvd. After crossing over the creek, turn left on Pine Dr, and left on the dirt road ½ mile further. The trailhead lies past the railroad tracks.

WHAT ELSE:

The Air Force Academy draws more than a million visitors a year. Most of them want to see the Cadet Chapel, with its soaring spires and windows overlooking the mountains. The chapel took five years to design, and another four to build.

All service a traveler would need can be found in Colorado Springs, just to the south of the Academy.

TRAIL: *Rock Island Trail / Falcon to Peyton*
DISTANCE: *9.0 miles*
SURFACE: *sand and gravel*
DIFFICULTY: *easy*

In the latter half of the 19th century, railroads dominated the country's transportation systems. Tracks were laid across the land, connecting far corners of the growing United States, moving people and freight. Many rail companies sprung up to service the growing population in the Midwest.

One company began operation in October 1852, running from Chicago to Joliet, IL. With no turntables in Joliet, the train had to make its return run in reverse! From this inauspicious opening, the Chicago and Rock Island Railroad (later the Chicago, Rock Island & Pacific RR) grew into one of the Midwest's largest railroads. Building many lines and acquiring others, it branched into states throughout the region. The first Rock Island tracks reached Colorado Springs on November 5, 1888.

One hundred years later, autos dominate the country's transportation system. Unable to compete, the Rock Island line went out of business in 1980. Competing railroads took over some of the abandoned tracks; others went into the public trust. With today's clamor for recreation facilities, many people have pushed to re-open those corridors as rails-to-trails conversions (RTCs).

One particular RTC opens up a bit of Colorado's plains, letting the rider escape the traffic on US24. However, it competes with the wide shoulders on US24. The highway gives the bicyclist a lot of room, and the hard surface allows higher speeds. Since the sand on the trail is sometimes fairly thick, I cannot recommend this trail for skinny tire bikes. Still, it is not technically difficult (flat its entire length), and does provide a diversion for the biker, walker, or horseback rider who doesn't like traffic whizzing by.

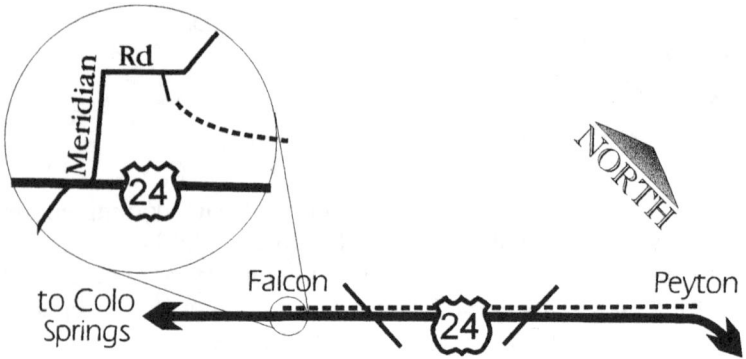

The northeast terminus of this trail is on the edge of Peyton, across the street from the post office. The trail lies on the old Rock Island Railroad bed, mere yards from US24. You will find no trees to shade you from the sun, so get started early on summer days.

The trail surface is sand, and hoofprints from the many horses may make the going bumpy. It stays on the sand except at the road crossings: Elbert Rd (3.7 miles) and Judge Orr Rd (7.0). The views of Pikes Peak and the neighboring mountains are spectacular, with no buildings or hills to interfere. You pass by an occasional house; otherwise the land is open fields.

The trail currently ends (9.0) at a newly-developed park in Falcon, located off Meridian Road. Being new, facilities are limited but are being developed.

Current plans call for extending the trail twelve miles along the corridor, hooking up to the Rock Island Trail inside Colorado Springs. As always, money and property issues will likely delay that from happening, but we can hope for someday!

WHAT ELSE:

Falcon and Peyton are small towns, where the convenience store is the center of activity. For lodging and restaurants, head into Colorado Springs for a wide selection.

TRAIL:	*Fountain Creek / Fountain to Colorado Springs*
DISTANCE:	*11.4 miles*
SURFACE:	*dirt/crushed gravel*
DIFFICULTY:	*easy to moderate -- a few small hills*

Fountain Creek is typical of many of the creeks draining the foothills and plains of Colorado. Early settlers aimed their wagons at them, seeing their sentinel lines of trees standing out on the barren prairie. Often, though, they would find the creeks dry, their waters running only in spring or after rains.

Today many of the streams run year-round. Some are dammed upstream, providing a constant flow for irrigation. More often, the increased flow results from the habits of the people moving in. Streets funnel city runoffs into the channels, and water from the thousands of lawns being sprinkled seeps is way into the streams.

On the plus side, stream beds make good candidates for open spaces. Trails, such as the one following Fountain Creek, provide access to the wonders of nature for those city dwellers.

This trail begins in Fountain at the Hanson Nature Park, Grinde Dr north of Lyckman Dr. From the parking area, follow the trail into the woods in the bottomland of the creek. The sandy trail runs upstream into Fountain Creek Regional Park, shaded under the leafy canopy.

At 1.1 miles the path branches. The right fork is considered an access road, following a canal by the side of a developed portion of the regional park before merging with the main path. Keep to the left instead, and follow the creek as it meanders north.

After the two paths rejoin (1.6), you pass the Duckwood trailhead of the regional park, another option for parking and beginning your ride. Again the path splits, with the right branch designated the service road. Again keep left on the main path, in the trees along the creek.

The two paths merge (2.0) at a trailhead for the Cattail

91

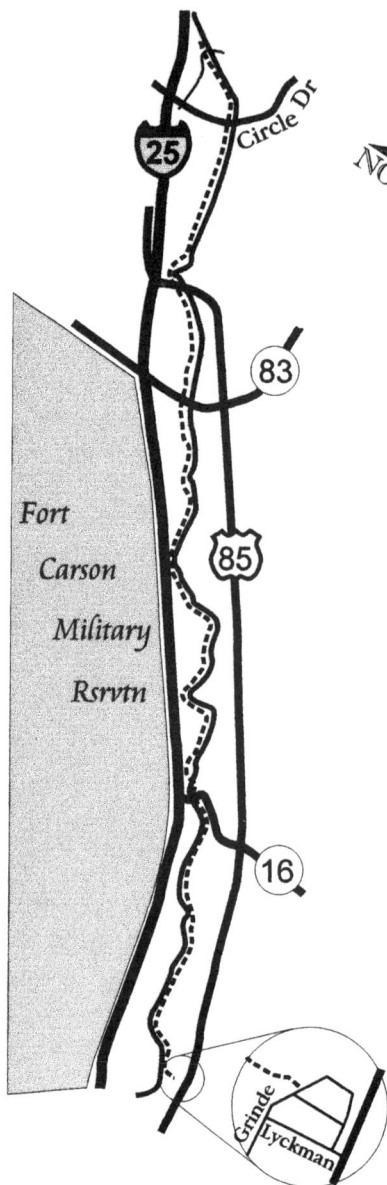

Marsh. This wild area offers a nature walk loop of 0.6 miles, but you'll have to hoof it – no bikes allowed. If you have the time, slow down and take the stroll.

The ride north through the regional park is a pleasure. Abundant trees and the ever-close creek give the trail a decidedly rural atmosphere, despite the city a few miles away. The only drawback may be the crowds sharing the trail, especially after passing the Willow Springs trailhead (2.8). Ahead lies a large picnic area and pond which attracts many families. Follow the trail over a small canal and around either side of the pond to again find a well-marked path.

Once under CO16 (3.3), you have left the regional park. This short stretch of trail is narrow and sandy, running behind a handful of yards. Quickly it rises above the creek to cross it (3.6) and leave the houses behind. On the opposite side the trail is again well-maintained.

The character of the trail has now changed. Instead of winding through the trees of the bottomland, the trail rolls through the near-treeless plains above the creek. Occasionally it dips to creek level, then climbs back out – a bit of a workout! To the west views run to the hills of Fort Carson, with I-25 cutting along their base. As it follows Fountain Creek's winding course, the trail nearly hits the interstate twice.

After miles through this mostly open territory, you reach houses again (7.3). After passing between back yards and the creek, the trail drops to pass under CO83 (7.7). For a bit you share the bottomland with a mobile home park, then head into thicker woods (8.3).

After riding under US85 (8.9) and past the adjacent trailhead, you reach the last main stretch of wild. Untouched nature ends at mile 10.0, where a new park complex was being developed in early 1999. Currently the trail skirts the site, staying close to the trees until ducking under Circle Dr (10.6).

Here the paved trail looks less maintained, with a layer of dirt on the blacktop. Though the bottomland has been left undeveloped, industry is close-by. Janitell Rd passes overhead at 11.2, and the trail ends unceremoniously (11.4) where Spring Creek joins Fountain Creek. Somewhere in the trees across the creek, Colorado Springs's Monument/Fountain Creek trail picks up the thread. How long before they are connected?

WHAT ELSE:

The northern end of this trail passes under Circle Dr. If you follow this road west, you come to the ritzy resort of the Broadmoor, one of the state's premier hotel complexes. Cheyenne Mountain Zoo perches above the resort; the country's only zoo situated on the side of the mountain.

All services are available in the metro area.

TRAIL: *Arkansas River & Fountain Creek / Pueblo*
DISTANCE: *11.3 miles*
SURFACE: *paved, concrete, dirt*
DIFFICULTY: *easy*

Pueblo's history is based on heavy industry. It first grew up as a rail center, funneling gold and silver from the mountain mines and coal from the deposits at Trinidad to markets back east. Colorado Fuel & Iron Company and other ironmakers opened smelters in the 1880's, establishing Pueblo as a steel town. Through the 1940's only Denver boasted more people in the state. Unfortunately an industry downturn devastated Pueblo in the 80's, as the mills laid off thousands of people.

With the steel came the magnates, building stately Victorian mansions in town. In other towns, a tear-'em-down-and-start-over fever has resulted in the loss of many such historic buildings. In Pueblo, it didn't, largely because there was no money left in the economy to do so. Now that the town has recovered, it has recognized its treasures and is working to maintain them. It now aggressively markets its charms and touts civic improvements – such as the Arkansas Riverwalk.

The Arkansas River and Fountain Creek provide a water 'skeleton' for the town. In the 1970's, the same time that Denver began to develop the Platte River bike network, the city started trails along its waterways. Now those trails reach from Lake Pueblo in the west to the University of Southern Colorado in the northeast.

We start this ride from the Greenway and Nature Center of Pueblo (see the Lake Pueblo ride for directions). From the park center, follow the trail between the river and buttes, then by an open space marked 'Southern Colorado Charros Association'. This space, which looks like an abandoned rodeo complex, is followed by more of the river woodlands.

At mile 0.8 a side spur heads north toward Nature Center Dr, but the main path crosses under Pueblo Blvd/CO45. It

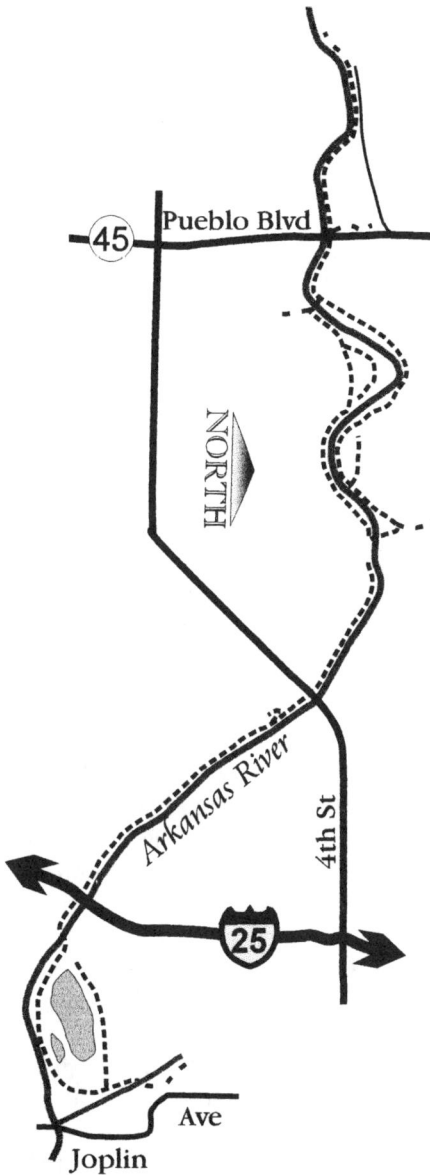

branches again at mile 1.1, with forks running along opposite sides of the river. I recommend crossing over the Arkansas and riding on the south side, which is very well marked. If you stay on the north, the trail merges with a road (1.7) before diverging again just over the railroad tracks (1.8). That trail then ends (2.5), and you must follow the dirt road away from the river toward Wildhorse Creek Park, then double back on the next dirt road to a trailhead and bridge.

If you cross over at the first junction, the path gives a second option once over the bridge. You can bear to the right and climb to City Park, or you can bear left toward downtown. The trail continues through river woodlands, with one loop following the river closely through a bend.

The woodlands end near the bridge connecting to Wildhorse

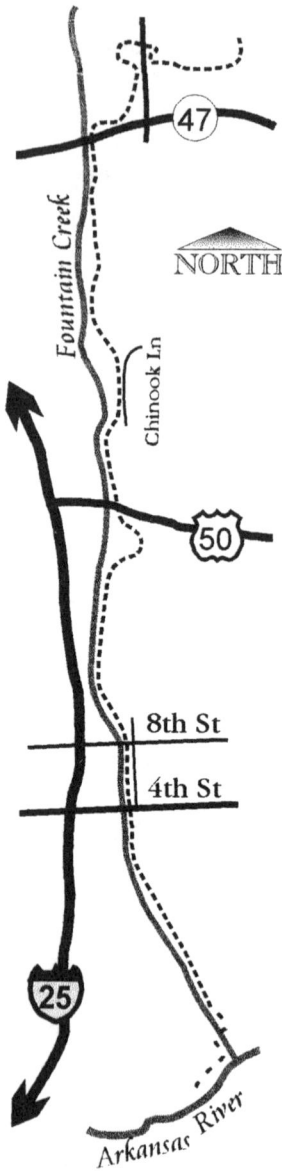

Creek Park (2.9). The river promptly enters a concrete-lined stretch, taming the dammed river. However, the city has turned this from a bleak, graffiti-strewn, urban wasteland into a gallery. Across the river artists have used the concrete walls as a canvas, filling it with oversized portraits, cartoons, logos, landscapes, and flights of fancy. Ever seen Jerry Garcia with bunny ears? He's here.

The trail here shows its age, with frost heaves making for a bumpy ride. We now head into downtown, crossing under 4th St/CO96 (3.6) and rising to a neighborhood connection (4.4) after passing most of the murals. After dropping back down, the murals suddenly reappear (4.8), but they are on our side, much too close to appreciate.

Once the trail passes under I-25 (5.0), it crosses over the river (5.1) and changes to a smoother concrete surface. The trail splits to circle the ponds (5.2), with both trails rejoining on the far side (5.8). I recommend the right side through the trees, rather than riding by the parking area. At 6.0 miles the trail sails over the railroad tracks, followed by a bridge over Fountain Creek (6.2).

From the adjacent trailhead (6.3), the path turns north to follow Fountain Creek. It varies between running through the bottomland and atop the levee. From the levee, you can catch glimpses of the city and I-25, and possibly a train chugging by across the creek. You reach the edge of downtown as you pass under 4th St (7.8). To your right now is a pocket park on Erie Ave, an alternate place to park and begin your ride.

Shortly after passing under 8th St, the smooth concrete portion of the trail ends (8.3). The open area above the creek grows more wild after passing under US50 (8.8), but then leaves the trees to run alongside Chinook Ln (9.2) and another city park. Following the creek north it passes under CO47 (10.3), then cuts back to approach Jerry Murphy Rd.

As of early 1999, this is a good place to turn back. The remaining trail has little to offer. After paralleling Jerry Murphy, it veers back toward the creek then passes through a pipe under the street (10.8). The trail now heads toward USC up a side gully, but doesn't quite reach it. It finally dead ends (11.3) at a spot where mountain bike paths begin behind a subdivision.

WHAT ELSE:

For many people, a summer wouldn't be complete without coming to Pueblo to attend the Colorado State Fair. For seventeen days city slickers and cowboys come for stock shows, rodeos, fiestas, and top national rock and country music bands.

The city offers a wide range of restaurants and lodging, but make reservations if you come during the Fair. Things get very crowded.

TRAIL: *Arkansas River & Lake Pueblo State Park*
DISTANCE: *8.1 or 8.4 miles*
SURFACE: *concrete, paved*
DIFFICULTY: *moderate - hilly section in the park*

The land around Lake Pueblo matches that found in many western films – limestone cliffs, buttes, scrubby semi-arid plains. If not for the backdrop of Pikes Peak and the Wet Mountains, a person could mistake it for a scene along the Mexican border. In fact, it used to lie on the Mexican border. Until the Mexican War in the 1840's, the Arkansas River separated the US from its southern neighbor.

In the early 1970's, the Bureau of Reclamation dammed the river for flood control and water supplies. The resulting lake – one of the state's largest – became a popular state park and recreational area. Sixty miles of shoreline wind around the lake, with the south shore accessible only by boat or hiking. Camping, fishing, and windsurfing attract crowds to the area. Of course, bicycling is also recommended, with a paved trail linking the park to the town.

This ride starts at the Greenway and Nature Center of Pueblo, located off Nature Center Drive west of Pueblo Blvd/CO45. (Take 4th St/CO96 west three-and-a-half miles from I-25, then north one mile on CO45.) The environmental park offers refreshments and bike rentals, and walking trails explore the adjacent wetlands. Next door, Pueblo's Raptor Center rehabilitates eagles and hawks and returns them to the wild.

From the Nature Center head west along the road or on the path by the bike rentals. The two routes merge at the park's edge (0.3 miles). The concrete trail that picks up – well-used by roller bladers – runs past 'old west' cliffs on the north. Try not to focus on the gravel mounds filling the land behind the fence on the south.

A bridge (1.6) takes you off concrete onto a blacktop path through a secluded picnic area, with trees providing shade from

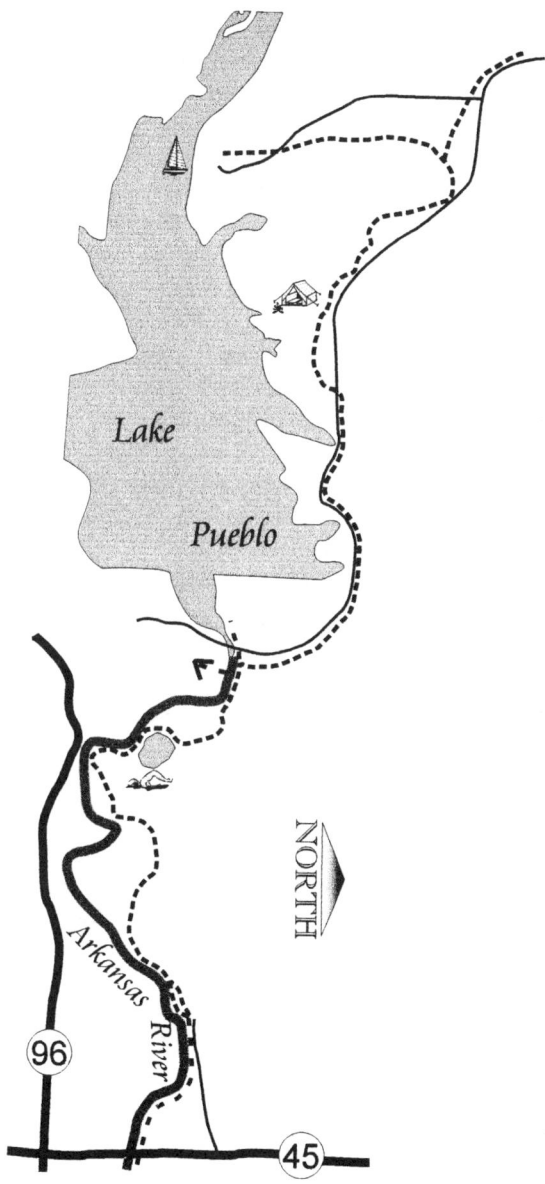

the summer sun. This lasts until you cross the park road (2.0), when you find yourself next to the Arkansas River. Soon the trail veers away to join another popular day use area surrounding a fishing pond. Parking is also available here if the Nature Center is full.

Follow the path around the pond, breaking away from the water at mile 2.7. The trail now loops back toward the river, passing beside a water park (a local swimming hole, since swimming is not allowed in Lake Pueblo). Ignore the trail spur to the left at 3.1, which crosses the river – you must stay on this side to ride through the park. Do take the right branch that immediately follows (3.3), as the straight-ahead path ends at the dam.

You can see the dam on your left as you enter the state park, giving you an idea of how far you must climb. Unfortunately, it does not climb gradually, but saves most of the gain for the very last (4.0). The reservoir comes into sight rapidly (4.1), but that doesn't mean you're done climbing. The trail (and the park road you shadow) continue like a roller coaster until reaching the 'top' at mile 5.2.

After crossing the park road (5.4), the land levels off. You zip by a campground (5.7) as you follow the path through trees and over the prairie. To the south the lake sparkles in the Colorado sun, and the Wet Mountains and Pikes Peak provide a backdrop for the scene. Be careful of your speed through the park – the path makes tight curves, and sand on the path could affect your control.

At mile 7.0 the trail crosses a gully on a narrow ledge attached to the road – signs urge you to dismount. On the other side you soon reach another trail fork (7.3). The right branch runs another 0.8 miles over prairie to the edge of the park; the left goes 1.1 miles as it drops down to the marina. Both spurs end at that point, and you return the way you came.

WHAT ELSE:

One of the state's largest bodies of water is also one of the state's most popular recreation destinations. Fishing, boating, and windsurfing all attract visitors. Camping is available in the park. For other services, Pueblo is located a short distance away.

COLORADO SPRINGS

In 1871 General William Jackson Palmer, a civil war hero who owned the Denver & Rio Grande Railroad, decided the area at the foot of Pikes Peak would serve as an excellent spot for a posh resort and home for his blue-blood bride, Queen Mellon. With splendid rock formations, waterfalls, and caves nearby, he saw it as a perfect area to settle. Unfortunately his mate had other ideas, and left after only a year for the civility of the east.

Today, the resort he started has become Colorado's second largest city. Fittingly, it also hosts the second-most developed trail network in the state. Though some of the trails do not link to others, the master plan envisions a network connecting all points of the city. Next up on the list is a four-mile trail between Platte Ave (US24) and Fountain Creek in the city's southeast corner.

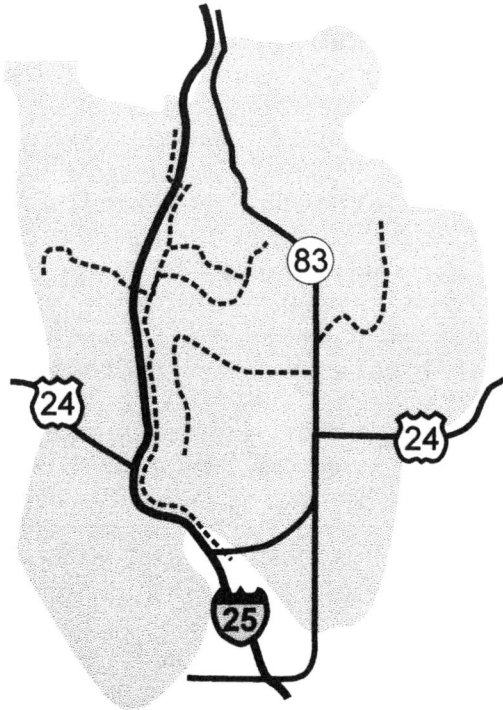

TRAIL: *Monument & Fountain Creeks*
DISTANCE: *11.8 miles*
SURFACE: *paved, dirt*
DIFFICULTY: *easy*

Monument Creek provides a backbone of sorts for Colorado Springs. Splitting the city on a north-south axis, it flows through residential neighborhoods, skirts the edge of downtown, and passes industry. Greenbelts and city parks run along most of its length, retaining a bit of nature in the middle of the urban grid.

The city's main trail follows the creek as it divides the city, running to its junction with Fountain Creek and continuing toward the southern city limits. This trail may soon join with the corresponding trails to the north and south, providing an off-street link between Palmer Lake and Fountain. A bridge connecting it to the Fountain/Security branch is planned for July 1999. In the north, officials hope to complete property negotiations and add the last one-mile link to the Air Force Academy into the network.

Currently, the trail begins in the north at Woodmen Rd and Corporate Dr, immediately west of I-25. From the parking area above the creek, cross Mark Dabling Blvd onto the smooth blacktop trail. It stays at street level, looking down on Monument Creek. A quick detour onto Corporate Dr (mile 0.3) gets you across a feeder stream, and the trail then jogs back east to regain the creek.

The trail crosses the creek at mile 1.1 (look for the big 'Bicycles' sign towering over the interstate here), and drops to creek level. The trail surface grows rough as you enter a strip wilder than before. I-25 passes overhead soon (1.5), and you shoot over the creek twice (2.0, 2.5). Riverbed plants and trees accompany you as the trail turns back and forth between dirt and pavement.

After passing under the Garden of the Gods Rd (2.9), you come upon a fishing pond. From here, you can cross over the

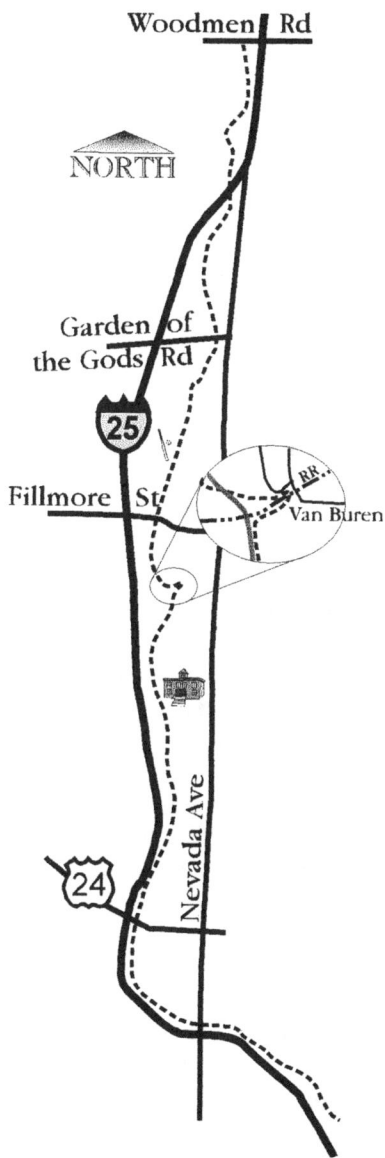

creek on the sidewalk and try the Austin Bluffs Trail, or continue down this trail. The trail strays a bit further above the creek, rising to street level right before reaching the Goose Gossage Youth Sports Complex (3.6). Straight ahead of you, the skateboard park attracts a good share of area youth. A bit further on, ballfields provide a venue for organized sports.

At mile 4.3, different trails merge. Across Mark Dabling, a trail heads east up Sinton Draw, running to Garden of the Gods Rd and connecting to the Foothills Trail. If you cross the bridge to your left, you will end up on the Templeton Gap Trail. Our trail, however, continues straight ahead.

The trail dives under Fillmore St (4.8) into another wild strip. Soon you're pedaling between neighborhoods, crossing Polk St (5.1) before the trail turns into a boardwalk and finally, sand. It dumps you onto Van Buren St, right on the Rock Island Railroad tracks. Don't get lost here! Make two right turns to cross the track, then double back west to Monument Creek.

The trail on the east side of the creek is now hard-packed dirt as it enters Monument Valley Park (5.8). Woods, picnic tables, ball and soccer fields, playgrounds, and walking trails fill this long park. Located just outside downtown and adjacent to Colorado College, it attracts scores of visitors. Keep your speed down as you traverse the park.

The trail dips under Uintah St (7.0), then crosses Cache la Poudre St/Mesa Rd on the south side of the CC campus. You finally leave Monument Valley Park at mile 8.0 as you drop to creek level to pass under Bijou St. Without the help of a bridge, cross the creek (8.2) and pass under Colorado Ave (8.4) before again rising out of the creek bed.

The trail continues under Cimmaron St (8.8) as it closely parallels I-25. Though the highway is often out of sight above you, you cannot escape the dull roar of the traffic. An intersecting trail at mile 9.2 marks the appearance of Fountain Creek. A right turn here takes you under the freeway and up to the edge of Bear Creek Regional Park; instead, turn left and cross the bridge over the creek.

The trail here, often switching between dirt and pavement, runs through the Tejon Wetlands. Wildlife frequents this stretch. If you have the time, posted maps show you the way to the viewing blinds.

At mile 10.0 the trail passes under Tejon St. The branch on the left empties into Dorchester Park with picnic tables and playgrounds (and restrooms, if nature is calling). To the right the path continues under Nevada Ave (10.1), then crosses (10.4) and recrosses (11.0) the creek.

As you continue, the land grows wilder, and you leave the heart of the city behind. After passing under US24 (11.4 - 11.5), the trail parts from I-25, and the traffic roar dies down. More trees shade your way as you coast to the current trail's end (11.8). Soon, though, a bridge will connect you to the next trail, letting you cycle all the way to Fountain.

TRAIL:	*Sinton Trail / Foothills Trail*
DISTANCE:	*3.7 miles*
SURFACE:	*paved*
DIFFICULTY:	*moderate*

If you're looking for a long ride on a scenic trail, forget about Sinton/Foothills. If you want to take the family out on a leisurely ride, look elsewhere. These trails are not as heavily used as many in the city, and have less to recommend them.

However, they are included here because they form an important link in the city's bike path network. From the greenway along Monument Creek, the Sinton Trail heads into the western foothills. Connecting with the Foothills Trail after a short section of city street, it provides access to Garden of the Gods. Why drive to the park, when you can exercise while getting there?

The Sinton Trail heads west from Monument Creek in the Goose Gossage Youth Sports Complex, on Mark Dabling Dr ½ mile north of Fillmore. (In the Monument Creek writeup, the branch is at mile 4.3.) On the north side of the stream, follow the path through an undeveloped area under the railroad tracks and Sinton Rd (0.3 miles). It curves around the business located there, and joins Ellston St (0.4) to pass under I-25.

Ellston ends at Chestnut St. Jog left to pick up the trail, a rough stretch of blacktop through the Douglas Creek open space. This section retains a wild feeling, filled with native vegetation. As you ascend the creek, it grows less wild. After crossing Holland Park Blvd (1.2), only the creek itself stays wild. Beyond the tunnel under Centennial Blvd (1.4), even the creek is shackled in concrete.

The rest of the Sinton Trail is a smooth blacktop path behind high-tech businesses along Garden of the Gods Rd and across the ditch from condos. Suddenly it breaks to the right to dump onto Garden of the Gods Rd opposite the gate to Hewlett-Packard. The city will extend the Sinton Trail to 30th St when the

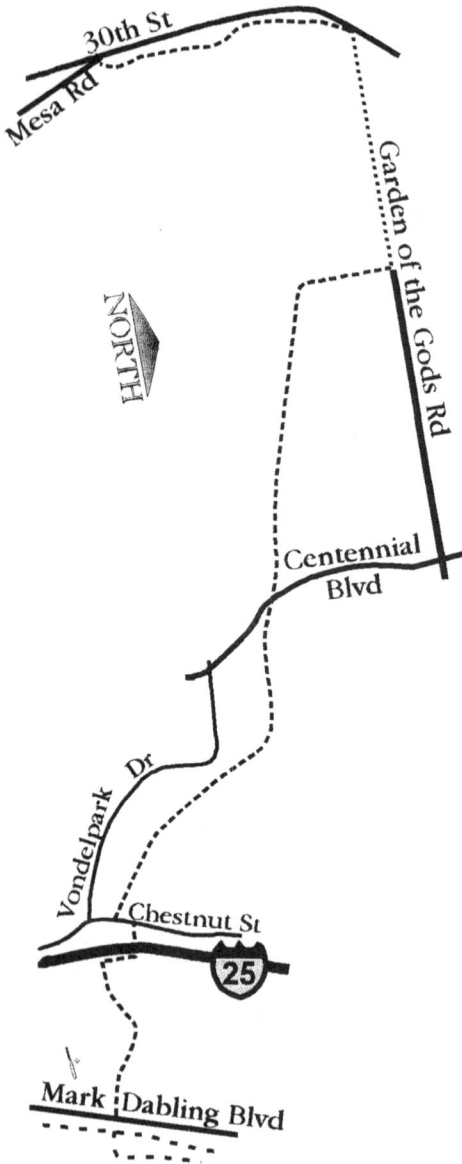

land ahead is developed, but for now you must detour to the street.

Follow Garden of the Gods Rd west to 30th (3.0), then join the impromptu path on the right side of 30th. The paved Foothill Trail soon takes over (3.1), climbing and then dropping as it parallels the road. After passing a trailhead at mile 3.5, the trail ends at Mesa Rd (3.7). Garden of the Gods park is a short distance further along 30th St.

WHAT ELSE:

From the junction of Mesa and 30th, Garden of the Gods Park lies just ahead. This free park with twisting rock needles and thousand-year-old juniper ranks as a top city attraction. Take time to see it, but beware the summer crowds.

TRAIL:	*Templeton Gap Trail / Austin Bluffs Trail*
DISTANCE:	*7.2 - 8.8 miles*
SURFACE:	*mostly paved or concrete*
DIFFICULTY:	*moderate – hills on Austin Bluffs*

Colorado Springs has developed a web of bike paths. Some follow area creeks, others shadow old rail lines, and still others run along ridges. Many connect with each other, allowing options for long rides. Only one pair, though, currently gives an option for an off-street loop.

The Templeton Gap and Austin Bluff trails open a swatch of north-central Colorado Springs to bicyclists. Along with a short length of the Monument Creek trail, it connects the city's University of Colorado branch with the greenway stretching through the heart of the city. Templeton Gap also ranks as the city's oldest bike path, dating to the mid-1980s.

Being a loop trail, you can begin at any point and head either direction. For easiest navigation I recommend a clockwise route, and I always prefer to get the hardest riding – the hills on Austin bluff – done first. Given that, start logging your miles as you leave the Monument Creek trail at Garden of the Gods Rd (mile 2.9 on that writeup).

South of Garden of the Gods Rd lies a fishing pond. Instead of dropping to pass under the road, stay high and cut between the concrete barriers to reach the sidewalk (mile 0.0). Head east (right) on the sidewalk to the intersection with Nevada Ave (0.2). Use the traffic lights to cross both streets to the northeast corner, where the Austin Bluff trail officially begins.

The trail parallels Austin Bluff Pkwy as it climbs a shallow hill. To your north, trees and prairie grasses fill a wide open strip. You will cross two quiet side streets (0.8, 1.0) before cresting the hill. As you pedal uphill, focus on the tree-covered hills ahead of you, and be thankful you don't need to climb them.

Watch your speed as the trail turns downhill. The university

lurks ahead, after you round a bend, and you may encounter student traffic. The university itself is tucked into the base of the hill, separated from the trail by a series of parking lots. Stop lights at miles 1.4 and 1.6 control the traffic in and out, so be prepared to stop.

The trail leaves the campus behind and transits a short wild stretch before turning downhill again. The slope picks up as you cross Cragmor Village Rd (1.9, again at 2.1), running past office buildings before jogging left to tunnel under Union Blvd (2.4). The Austin Bluff trail then ends, joining the Templeton Gap trail.

The TG trail here runs both directions along a concrete floodway. For a slightly longer ride, turn left and climb above the concrete ditch, following Union as it heads north. Wooded hills rise to your right, the greenery interrupted by an occasional house. The waterway eventually goes subterranean (3.1), and the trail ends (3.2) when it reaches Garden Ranch Dr. Turn around and follow the trail back, skipping the first trail to pass under Austin Bluffs Pkwy (4.0).

The hills of Palmer Park now rise to the east. (This patch of wilderness-in-the-city is well worth checking out, with picnic sites, scenic overlooks, and mountain bike trails weaving through the hills.) Across the creek from the trail, the houses sit on large lots, and you may see horses in the stables. Soon the concrete lining the trail ends (4.6), replaced by rock levees. The greenbelt strip between the creek and road also widens at this point.

The trail reaches Union at mile 4.9, joining the sidewalk to cross over the creek. A trail now stretches back along the opposite bank of the ditch; take it, but quickly branch right to tunnel under Union. The trail on this side turns to dirt; use the sidewalk to cross over the creek to the paved path on the north side.

This path ends at Hancock Ave (5.4). You must pedal through the parking lot of Portal Park to find the continuation. It then passes by construction as it follows the ditch, now filled with wetland grasses in its wide bed. This stretch lasts until dropping onto Montview Ln (6.5) at Nevada Ave.

Turn left on Nevada at the light, and immediately catch the trail on the creek's south bank. This will take you down to Monument Creek, with an impressive view of the mountains ahead of you. Due to more construction, the pavement ends (6.8) shy of the creek. Head to the left (south), even though the heavy equipment has erased most signs of the trail here. In a short time the trail appears again (7.1), a dirt path that drops into the creek's bottomlands before climbing out and crossing a bridge (7.4) into the Goose Gossage Youth Sports Complex.

Catch the Monument Creek trail on the west side of the bridge, and follow it north. The paved trail turns to dirt as it reaches the fishing pond at Garden of the Gods Rd. Ahead is the entrance to the sidewalk (8.8), which marks the completion of your loop.

TRAIL: *Rock Island Trail / Shook's Run Trail*
DISTANCE: *6.8 miles*
SURFACE: *paved*
DIFFICULTY: *easy*

"One day some of the other teachers and I decided to go on a trip to 14,000-foot Pikes Peak. We hired a prairie wagon. Near the top we had to leave the wagon and go the rest of the way on mules. I was very tired. But when I saw the view, I felt great joy. All the wonder of America seemed displayed there, with the sea-like expanse."

So wrote Katharine Lee Bates in 1893 as she spent her summer in Colorado Springs. Inspired by the view from Pikes Peak, she wrote a poem immortalizing what she saw. Her poem was printed in a weekly journal on July 4, 1895, and quickly became famous. "America the Beautiful" captured the nation's heart, and people lobbied to name it our national anthem. Today many still consider it the best song to represent the country.

To celebrate the land that inspired the song, public officials have designated an "America the Beautiful" trail. Many sections of the proposed trail have yet to be established, but it does include trails already running through El Paso County and Colorado Springs. The Rock Island trail is one of those, providing spectacular views to the mountains.

Start this ride on Academy Blvd at Maizeland Rd, at the southeastern corner of Palmer Park. Homestead Ridge Trail ends one block east of here, if you wish to connect for a longer ride. However, our ride heads south in the center median of Academy, rolling along on smooth blacktop under the power lines. Beware of the one street that crosses the median (0.3 miles) – the curb is sharp, a big surprise if you don't expect it.

The median trail ends at Constitution Ave (0.6). Use the crosswalk to cross Academy and then Constitution, and grab the Rock Island Trail over the railroad tracks. From here it

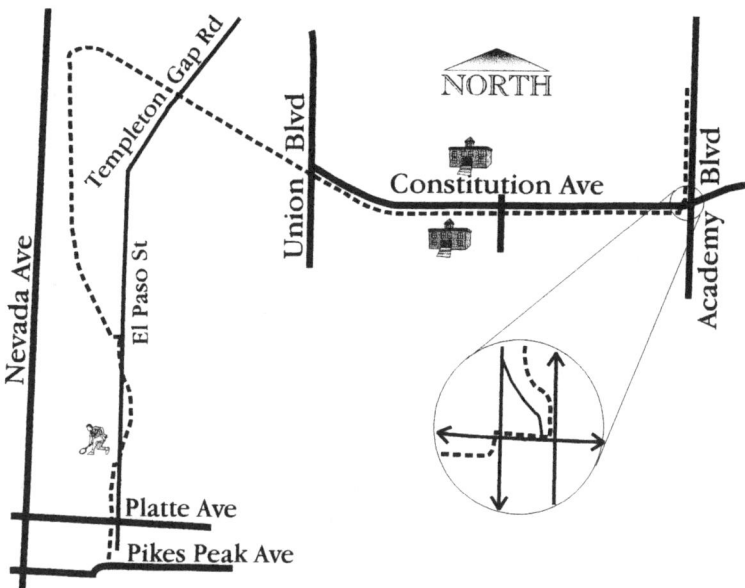

heads due west, paralleling Constitution but often hidden from it below the tracks. The level terrain guarantees an easy, quiet ride, broken up only by two street crossings: Chelton Rd (1.0) and Circle Dr (1.6).

After passing Wasson High and Jefferson Elementary schools, the trail and railroad bend to the northwest. Suddenly the houses lining the trail disappear, leaving a view that underlines Bates's lyrics. Rolling hills spread to the south, with slopes covered with houses and businesses. The greenery of a golf course lies ahead. At the base of the mountains, the rock formations of Garden of the Gods provide a red contrast to the greenery. Towering above it all is the summit of Pikes Peak.

After you cross Union Blvd (2.7), you skirt the Jewett Golf Course. Once again nothing blocks the spectacular views to the west. The trail continues straight ahead, crossing Paseo Rd (3.3) and Templeton Gap Rd (3.5). After Templeton Gap, the trail surface shows some neglect as it doubles as an alleyway for the houses to your left. The Rock Island trail finally ends (4.1) at a park on Weber & Lilac Sts.

To your left, Shook's Run Trail heads south toward downtown. It runs through a narrow grass strip beside Weber between businesses and houses, crossing numerous side streets. At Fontanero St (4.8), signs direct you to cross at the light at Wahsatch Ave. After Caramillo St (5.1), cross Wahsatch as the trail angles to the southeast.

Follow the bike route signs when you reach Uintah St (5.6), crossing at the light at El Paso St and staying on El Paso until the trail cuts away to the left. At 6.0 miles the trail crosses over Cache la Poudre St and enters North Shook's Run Park. You now follow this long, narrow park south, crossing several side streets and taking bridges over others. This greenbelt provides an antidote to the bustle of downtown a few blocks to the east.

Unfortunately, Shook's Run Trail does not yet connect to anything else. This stretch abruptly ends at Pikes Peak Ave (6.8). After a gap of several blocks, the trail picks up again to run through South Shook's Run Park, but that still stops short of Fountain Creek. There are plans to connect Shook's Run to the main greenway both in the north and south, but no definite timetables. At this time, you either have to navigate city streets to make a connection, or return the way you came.

TRAIL: *Homestead Ridge*
DISTANCE: *4.9 miles*
SURFACE: *paved, concrete, dirt*
DIFFICULTY: *moderate - many short hills*

Colorado Springs's trail system grows year by year, tying more of the city into the network of off-street paths. If all proposed paths on the current Parks & Recreation Facilities map were built, most of the city would lie within two miles of a bike path. At the present time, though, only one trail exists in the eastern part of the Springs.

The Homestead Trail, one of the oldest in town, runs through the houses of Homestead Ridge. Since it lies on or near the ridge line, it involves a bit of up and down riding. You can find great views along parts of the trail, but often it runs east of the ridge, blocking sight of the magnificent mountains.

On the north, the trail starts in the Old Farm subdivision. To reach it, take Garden of Gods Rd/Austin Bluffs Pkwy (exit 146 off I-25) east 5½ miles to Old Farm Dr. A right turn takes you to Old Farm Cir, and follow that left around the bend and past Old Farm Community Ctr. The trail starts opposite Silo Ridge.

Immediately the path enters a wild area atop the bluff. Yucca and scrub brush surround you, with houses spread out below you. The trail looks old, with sand blown over stretches of the rough blacktop.

You quickly descend out of the wild into a developed park with a playground. The trail runs south through the park, before 'ending' on Old Farm Cir. To continue, cross the street and follow Iron Horse Tr south. You will see the trail on your left, a dirt path (mile 0.5) climbing steeply up from the street. Downshift before hitting it, or you will end up walking.

Once again atop the ridge, the trail levels off, crossing a circle (0.8) bounded by Coneflower Ln and Bluestem Ln. On the far side the path becomes paved again, entering another wild stretch. The views here stretch to the east, over the hilly

113

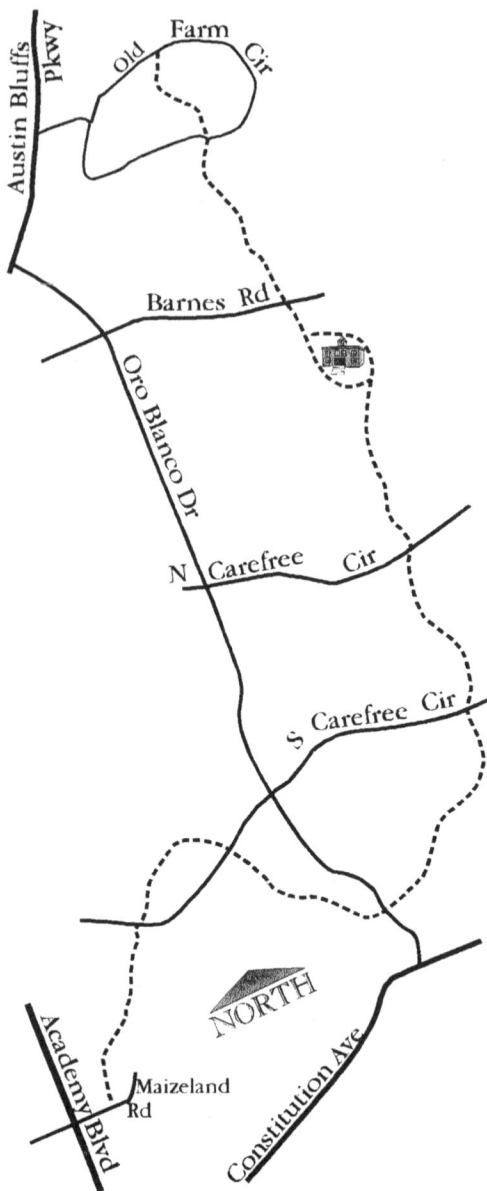

prairie.

Use the pedestrian light to cross Barnes Rd (1.1), where the trail turns to concrete. The path quickly branches to circle Rudy Elementary School; I recommend the left fork. It runs behind the school, above a slope filled with dirt paths for mountain bikes. Past the school, picnic tables and park benches provide a place to rest and gaze out over the eastern city.

Soon houses crowd the trail again. At mile 1.9 another pedestrian light helps you cross N Carefree Cir into another narrower wild strip. The trail crosses Whimsical Dr (2.3), and then passes a park with volleyball courts and a playground. One last pedestrian light helps you cross S Carefree

Cir (2.6).

The next short stretch of the trail grows rougher. Old blacktop turns into dirt and then back to blacktop, and it gets narrow in the middle. This only lasts until you cross Inspiration Dr (2.9), when it returns to concrete. After Oro Blanco Dr (3.4), rough blacktop takes over as you descend from the ridge. Watch your speed while you focus on the great views of Pikes Peak and surrounding mountains.

At S Carefree Cir (3.9) you have an option. The trail dips to pass under the street, but the tunnel may collect a layer of leaves, sticks, and trash. Instead, you can cross the street at the pedestrian light, and join the trail on the opposite side. From here the trail runs by Penrose Elementary School, then joins a concrete creek.

For the trail's final stretch, it loops back along the strip between the concrete creek and houses. After a bike- and bone-jarring crossing of the creek under S Carefree Cir (4.4), the path turns to a narrow dirt path between creek and fences. You reach Radiant Dr at mile 4.8, and turn left to reach Maizeland Rd (4.9).

The Homestead Trail ends here. The parks map shows a proposed extension along the concrete creek to Sand Creek at Platte Ave, but that project has no timetable. For the time being, you can pedal east to Academy Blvd and catch the Rock Island Trail toward downtown.

DENVER METRO AREA

Last (but certainly not least) comes Denver and the surrounding metropolis. The six-county metro area is home to more than half of the state's population, and hosts more than half of the state's recreation trails. With over 400 miles of paths weaving through the region, it's no wonder that *Bicycling* magazine named Denver as one of North America's '10 Best Cycling Cities' (March 1999 issue).

The climate in Denver encourages sports like skating, walking, and bicycling. Even during the dead of winter, snow rarely lasts, and dry, sunny days make it easy to get your exercise without spending your time in a club. This region has had a love affair with bikes for many years. In 1900, reported the Denver Post, the city had more bikes per residents than any other US city.

However, automobiles pushed bikes out of the spotlight, and many years passed with no

emphasis on trails. Isolated paths existed in widely-spaced parks, or ran a short distance along Cherry Creek, but no network existed. Then the South Platte River flooded in 1965, sparking interest in converting it from an eyesore to a public treasure – which included multi-use trails running its length.

In June 1974 Mayor Bill McNichols appointed Joe Shoemaker chairman of the Platte River Development Committee. With a few hand-picked members, he tackled the transformation of the river. City dumps became parks, and dams soon sported boat chutes. By mid-1975, the first segments of the Platte River had opened, followed by the dedication of Confluence Park that September.

Now twenty years have passed, and the network of trails ties the metropolitan area together. New trails, such as the Sand Creek Greenway, continue to sprout, and old ones get extended. No matter where you find yourself, you're never far from a trail.

Full coverage of Denver's trail system is beyond the scope of this book. In the following pages, then, are brief descriptions of the longest eleven trails in the metro area. For more detailed information and a wider selection of trails, please refer to *Take A Bike! A Guide to the Denver Area's Urban Bike Trails*. This book covers a wide sampling of many major trails in the city. (It can be obtained wherever *Trails Away / Colorado* is sold, or can be ordered directly from CAK Publishing. See the order blank on the final page.)

TRAIL:	*Bear Creek / Sheridan - Denver - Lakewood*
DISTANCE:	*13.6 miles*
SURFACE:	*paved*
DIFFICULTY:	*easy (along creek) to strenuous (around lake)*

Who says place names have to be unique?

Take Bear Creek, for example. At last count, thirty streams bore the name 'Bear Creek' – and that's just in Colorado. Though many may have earned their name, its doubtful many bears would be sighted along most of the creeks nowadays. Especially along the Bear Creek draining the foothills west of Denver.

The stream flowing through the southwestern suburbs is tamed by Bear Creek Dam. After escaping the confines of the reservoir, it meanders east through a string of parks and greenbelts, providing a welcome break in the dense cityscape. At its east end, it merges with the South Platte River near Hampden Ave (US285) and Santa Fe Dr (US85).

The trail follows the creek from its mouth to the point where it exits Bear Creek Canyon. Most of the trail runs through public parks. The best places to access the trail are Bear Creek Park (Sheridan Blvd south of Hampden Ave), Bear Valley Park (Dartmouth Ave between Sheridan and Wadsworth Blvds), and Bear Creek Lake Park. You may also connect the ride with a trip along the Platte River Trail.

Our trail leaves the Platte River on the north edge of Englewood Municipal Golf Course. After passing through a wild, brushy area, it enters the only 'urban' stretch of the path, with RV lots, storage lockers, and other businesses crowding the stream. At mile 1.4 you cross over the creek on Lowell Blvd, then finally leave the blight behind.

Mullen High School borders the trail to the south, then you enter Bear Creek Park. This is a good trail access, and offers picnic tables, playgrounds, and restrooms. Beware of pedestrian traffic!

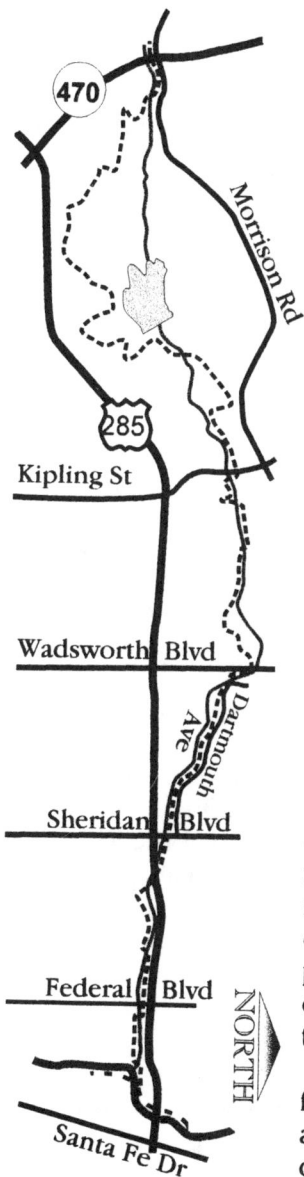

Bear Valley Shopping Center interrupts the greenery as the path follows the edge of the parking lot there. Bear Valley Park (mile 2.8) awaits as you leave that commercial strip, giving the rider an option. Signs here direct the biker looking for speed to the 'express lane' along Dartmouth Ave. For a more relaxed ride, you may stay on the trail as it winds through the long park. At 3.1 miles a perennial garden brightens the trail; take a break and see how many of the flowering plants you can name. After merging again with the 'fast lane', it leaves this park and crosses under Wadsworth Blvd (4.5).

You are now in the Bear Creek Greenbelt. The trail veers from the creek to run through a prairie grassland -- say 'hello' to the prairie dogs watching you pass. At 5.1 miles a spur to the south connects to Lakewood's Sister City Park; the main trail aims back toward the creek. A side path and bridge at 5.3 miles leads to Stone House Park; restrooms are available there. After crossing under Estes St, the path passes a horse training field before crossing the creek again to wind through an urban 'forest'.

When the greenbelt ends (6.2), follow the signs left over the creek, across quiet Kipling St and back down to the creek. After passing under Kipling Pkwy (6.5), the trail twists and curves past well-kept gardens of creek-side residents. The trail finally parts from the creek at 7.1 miles, veering to Morrison Rd, then following Owens Ln into Fox Hollow Golf Course (7.4). The road passes by the clubhouse before winding along the base of the dam, with a marked bike lane to keep you on track.

For a good workout, it's hard to beat this part of the trail. By the time you reach the golf course, pedestrian traffic has mostly disappeared. The climb up to the top of the dam starts at the maintenance buildings (8.6), and is one of the longest and steepest in the Denver area. Now get ready to shift into low gear as the trail starts its climb.

The trail edges south through a shadeless landscape covered with low plants. Soon it steepens, throwing switchbacks your way as it reaches for the summit. You can see bikers disappear around a far bend on the skyline, but when you reach it (9.4) you realize it is not yet the summit. Now the foothills tower over you to the west; far below to the south traffic zooms by on US285. The trail tops out at mile 10.0; a short spur to the right leads to a shaded table and some interpretive signs.

A steep downhill now greets you, but sharp turns force you to keep your speed down. The bottom of the hill arrives way too soon at 10.5 miles, after which the trail rises and falls over the rolling prairie. Several interpretive signs along the trail tell of the area's wildlife and history; stop and learn a little! You finally rejoin the creek bed at the park's west end, reaching a trail head on Morrison Rd at mile 13.4. After passing under C-470, the trail ends abruptly at mile 13.6. (For a longer ride, you can cross Morrison Rd and join the northern-most section of the Centennial Trail.)

WHAT ELSE:

Bear Creek Lake Park offers swimming and boating in the Soda Lakes, and a campground is open to the public.

TRAIL: *Centennial (C/E-470) Trail*

New highways are getting harder and harder to build.

As Colorado enters the new millennium, new highways grow scarce. Environmental laws, impact statements, and citizen activists make approving roads a long process – witness the long-proposed Northwest Parkway.

As a result, the C470 / E470 'ring road' (including the Northwest Parkway) may be the last major addition to Denver's highway network. This autobahn, part tollway and part freeway, circles the edges of the metro area – though the edges are already pushing beyond the highway. Perhaps the nicest part of the road is the fact that an adjoining bike path has been planned for its length.

Though the trail is not complete – construction of the path beside the newest stretches of toll road has not yet begun – it comprises an important piece of the area bike network. An intrepid bicyclist, by combining a portion of this Centennial Trail with the Platte River Greenway and the Cherry Creek Trail, can travel nearly fifty miles on trails. He can ride from Adams County to Parker without resorting to city streets.

Good trailheads for the Centennial Trail are few (who wants to build a park bordering a major highway?). One I recommend is to park at Writer's Vista Park (Mineral Ave between Broadway and Santa Fe Dr). From there, follow the Highline Canal Trail 1.3 miles south to reach the Centennial Trail.

WHAT ELSE:

This highway runs through a growing urban area, with services widely available. Chatfield State Park offers swimming, fishing, scuba diving, windsurfing, hiking, and birdwatching. For a different brand of sport, Park Meadows Mall offers shopping and people-watching in its faux-ski lodge setting.

121

TRAIL:	*Centennial Trail / Douglas County*
DISTANCE:	*12.9 miles*
SURFACE:	*paved*
DIFFICULTY:	*moderate – many small hills*

From the junction with Highline, head east onto the Centennial Trail and parallel the busy ribbon of Highway C470. A small fence and a few yards of vacant land separate you from traffic. Behind you the mountains rise above the cityscape, but the scenery surrounding you consists of grass, a few scraggly trees, asphalt parking lots and boxy shopping centers, and the ever-present traffic screaming by.

The trail seems to constantly rise as it heads east, with dips to cross the roads with freeway ramps – Broadway (mile 0.6); University Blvd (2.1). A trailhead awaits at Colorado Blvd (3.2), near a park for mountain bikers. Businesses seem to increase as you cross Quebec St (5.3), and you navigate a narrow strip between the freeway and Parkway Dr.

Park Meadows Shopping Center looms ahead when you reach Yosemite St (6.7). At the light, the trail crosses both Yosemite and Park Meadows Dr to run through a buffer zone south of the mall. It then dives under the I-25/C470 interchange, using a string of underpasses to clear the junction. At mile 8.1 you join Valley Hwy Rd to duck under E470; the trail starts again on the other side.

To the east, development has not yet filled the land (though it is growing). Office parks and golf courses keep company with open fields. You cross Peoria (9.5) and a toll plaza as the trail continues to climb and fall. After one rise, views of the Cherry Creek valley and Parker spread before you.

After crossing Jordan Rd (12.3), the trail ends (12.9) just shy of Parker Rd. The southern portion of the Cherry Creek Trail runs off in either direction, though the northern end lies only two miles to the left.

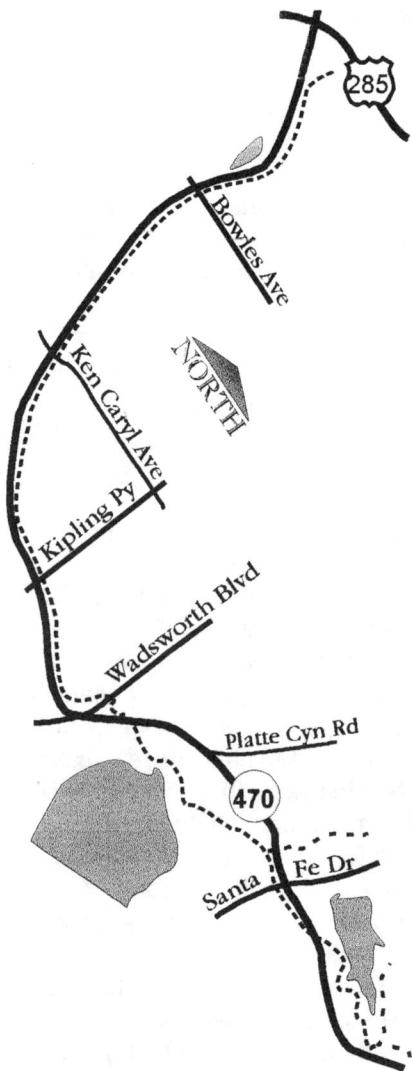

Centennial Trail SW

Centennial Trail E

TRAIL:	*Centennial Southwest / Jefferson & Douglas Counties*
DISTANCE:	*13.7 miles*
SURFACE:	*concrete, paved*
DIFFICULTY:	*moderate to strenuous*

From the junction with the Highline Canal, the trail follows the canal west, winding through open land while staying in sight of County Line Rd. After crossing under C470 (1.9 miles), the Highline Canal Trail continues straight ahead. The Centennial Trail branches to the right, crossing Santa Fe Dr (2.5) into Chatfield State Park. Follow it through a grove of trees past the Platte River Trail to a shaded picnic area (3.2). At this point you must join the park road to climb to the top of the dam (4.6). As you descend the other side, the trail quickly branches from the road (4.7) and crosses under C470.

Here the trail 'T's. To the right, the Columbine (Platte Canyon Rd) Trail takes you north into Littleton. Our trail parallels the highway as it heads west, briefly jogging north to cross under Wadsworth Blvd. Now the views are of distant condos, fields, and billboards as you travel to Kipling Ave (7.2).

New developments now border the ring road as it nears the foothills. After crossing Ken Caryl Rd (9.5), the 'Big Dip' awaits. The trail takes a long (appr. one mile) downhill cruise to pass West Meadows Golf Course, then follows with a longer climb back to Bowles Ave (11.8). If the sun is beating down while you're pedaling up, you can stop for an afternoon 'shade break' where the trail hugs a brick wall that holds in the freeway.

At Bowles Ave stop and look around. To the northwest a gap in the ridge reveals views of mountain peaks. A sea of houses fills the view to the southeast, and they crowd further west all the time. The trail passes some empty fields on its way to cross Belleview Ave (12.8), and finally ends at Quincy Ave and Eldridge St.

TRAIL:	*Cherry Creek / Denver*
DISTANCE:	*13.2 miles*
SURFACE:	*paved, concrete*
DIFFICULTY:	*easy to moderate (at the dam)*

In 1858, rival groups of settlers and prospectors formed two towns at the confluence of the South Platte River and a creek flowing in from the east. The first, named Auraria, was settled by the first prospectors to find gold on the South Platte. North of the creek, Gen. William Larimer founded a camp with a group he led from Leavenworth, KS. Since Larimer had actually jumped another group's claim, he named his settlement after the territorial governor, hoping to enlist his help in settling the conflict. That governor was James W. Denver.

Now Cherry Creek forms the unofficial southern border of downtown Denver. Passing beneath the city's skyscrapers, it provides an oasis from the bustle of the city. Encased in a concrete canyon as it passes downtown, the stream bed widens as you move upstream. The urban portion of the waterway begins just outside Denver city limits, at the dam forming Cherry Creek Reservoir.

One of the city's most popular paths runs the length of the stream. From Confluence Park, where the waters empty into the Platte, to Denver Country Club, the trail runs beneath the walls of the concrete canyon. Often the trail user is out of sight to everyone but the motorists on Speer Blvd. Past Cherry Creek Shopping Center the trail winds through tree-filled stream beds or through groomed parks above the creek.

The trail splits from the Platte River Greenway at Confluence Park, crossing the river on the bridge above the boat chute. During many weekends, kayakers or inner-tubers pack this piece of the river, practicing their skills or just escaping the heat.

The trail follows the creek downtown, dropping into the greenway. Several historic railroad bridges pass by overhead,

125

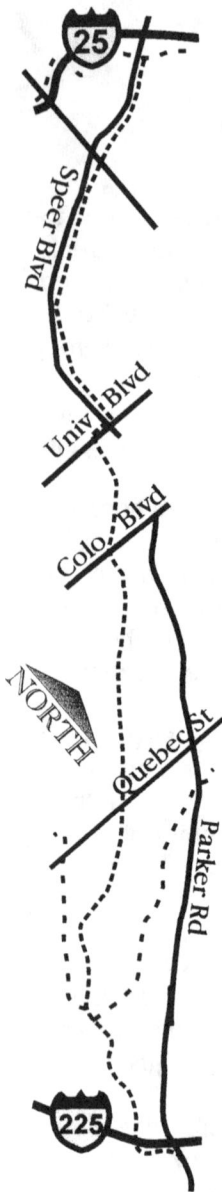

recalling Denver's history as a transportation hub. As you near Lower Downtown (LoDo), trail traffic increases. Through the most popular section the trail splits, with bikers and skaters directed to the south bank while hikers can amble on the north.

The greenway retains its tamed character throughout this stretch. The creek, boxed in by the walls below Speer Blvd, runs arrow-straight. Man-made cascades control the stream's level, removing rapids in favor of a consistent flow. Grass banks replace the sandy bluffs from upstream, and well-spaced trees dot the banks. An occasional sandbar or small grassy island appears in the stream. Still, it is a welcome refuge from the steel-and-glass forest above the creek.

At mile 3.5 it rises from its gulch to join the sidewalk in front of Denver Country Club. Following 1st Ave to University, it then turns right and crosses under University (4.3) to reach the shopping center. Stop here for refreshments or lunch, or continue into a more natural stream bed. The trail dips to creek level or below – beware of sand or water here if the creek runs high.

The paved trail climbs out of the creek at mile 4.8, while dirt walking trails continue to wind through the bottomlands. After a short jaunt through the industrial terrain of Glendale, you reenter Denver at Four-Mile House Park (6.3). Watch for Denver's oldest home, a tepee, and (if you're lucky) a stagecoach passing by. The creek's valley is wider here, with many foot trails close to the water.

Across Holly St (6.8) you enter Garland Park, then wiggle through a green swath guarded by utility towers. At the east end of Cook Park a bridge delivers you to the creek's south bank (7.9), and you quickly return to the creek bed to pass under Quebec. The trail then rises to street level again, losing sight of the creek as it disappears behind a chain link fence.

Follow the trail as it corkscrews under Iliff Ave (9.2) and over the creek. You now accompany the trail through a dusty western landscape as it runs between a subdivision and the Los Verdes Country Club. The trail merges with the Highline Canal (10.4), running east (left) for 0.1 miles. Follow the signs when the trails branch again; the creek should stay to your left.

Ahead of you now looms the earthen mass of Cherry Creek dam. Stay on the path through the open area and over a side creek (11.0), and then cross Cherry Creek a final time. Below the bridge you can see fringes of J. F. Kennedy Municipal Golf Course.

The trail crosses under Havana St @ Dartmouth Ave, then follows the edge on the golf course. At the Kennedy ballfields (11.9) the trail drops to cross under I-225 (12.2), then abruptly changes direction to UP! Downshift and climb up the side of the dam, counting every foot as you eagerly watch the trail approach the dam crest. The trail reaches Parker Rd then joins the sidewalk to cross Dam Crest Rd/Vaughn Way (13.2). Just after the traffic light, the trail enters Cherry Creek State Park, with its own network of hiking and cycling trails.

WHAT ELSE:

The trail provides access to downtown Denver, with LoDo, Larimer Square, and the 16th St Mall drawing visitors. Downstream, the Cherry Creek Shopping Center offers upscale shopping. Past the dam, the state park offers a variety of outdoor recreation.

TRAIL: *Cherry Creek Trail / Parker*
DISTANCE: *12.0 miles*
SURFACE: *paved*
DIFFICULTY: *easy*

There is more to Cherry Creek than a thin ribbon of water flowing by the skyscrapers of downtown Denver en route to the South Platte River. South of the city, the creek meanders through open terrain, sometimes bordering by houses, at others embraced by parkland. From Castlewood Canyon State Park outside Franktown to Cherry Creek State Park, it traverses a region with a distinct rural feel, though one that is seeing its share of Colorado's growth.

Another type of growth is taking place here. In one of the metro area's more ambitious plans, backers hope to link the above state parks with a recreational trail. Already fifteen of the twenty-four miles are in place, comprising three separate sections. The longest runs 12.0 miles, from the Douglas County line to the Pinery Country Club south of Parker.

The trail currently begins in the Cottonwood area of north Parker. From local parks, it follows the creek upstream, splitting the neighborhoods before it passes under Cottonwood Dr (mile 0.6) into open fields. (There is a trailhead with parking on Cottonwood.) Be sure to close the gates as you enter and leave the pasture.

After passing under E470 (1.4), the creek hosts a thick woodlands. Gone is the noise of traffic; in its place, listen to the birds calling (or the wind whistling). To the west, the peaks of the Front Range rise above the nearby hills. The remote feel continues as you pass under Lincoln Ave (2.7) in Challenger Regional Park.

After crossing the creek, you wheel by the charred buildings of a fireman training facility. The creek remains filled with trees as you work your way upstream, shading you on hot summer days. Parker's Main St crosses overhead (4.0) just before

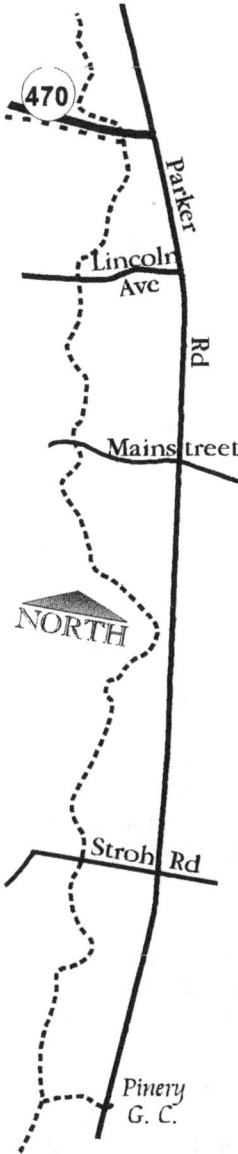

reaching Bar CCC Park, another good trailhead. The Sulphur Gulch Trail branches here and heads east into town; the Cherry Creek Trail crosses the bridge and continues south.

The trail continues in open spaces until reaching Parker Regional Park at Indian Pipe Ln & Country Meadows Dr (6.0). Now houses border you to the east as the creek darts in and out of view. Connections to the neighborhoods branch from the trail every quarter-mile or so until you pass under Stroh Rd (7.8) and leave the houses behind.

The land is now wide open, with cows and horses claiming fields as their own and the often-dry creek winding through a wild landscape. A picnic shelter in a grove of mature cottonwoods (8.4) provides a place to rest before tackling the rest of the trail.

The trail forks (11.4) as it nears its end. The left branch leads to the Pinery (12.0), while the main path continues to Scott Rd (12.0). As of 1998 under a mile separated this from the Castle Oaks segment, but no easy road connection exists.

WHAT ELSE:

Several creekside parks offer recreational opportunities. The nearby town of Parker offers many services, or you can travel up the road to Denver and its suburbs.

TRAIL:	*Clear Creek / Adams County - Wheatridge*
DISTANCE:	*13.6 (trail) + 1.2 (street) miles*
SURFACE:	*paved, concrete*
DIFFICULTY:	*easy*

Unlike Bear Creek to the south, Clear Creek has no flood control reservoir to temper its flow. As a result, its levels may vary more than its cousin to the south. Most of the parks along its length remain in a fairly natural state, without groomed lawns and facilities. However, portions of the accompanying trail have a grittier quality, running within sight of industry or by gravel pits (some reclaimed). Also, the trail is not yet continuous, with a 1.5 mile unmarked stretch on city streets needed to link the two halves.

The trail branches from the Platte River a the mouth of the creek. A waterside park off CO224 between Washington and York Sts provides access to the trail. Running along the wild creek bed, the concrete trail passes under the I-25/I-76 interchange (mile 1.8-2.0) and by businesses and houses. After passing a large pond, the surroundings turn industrial. The path crosses Pecos St (3.4) and joins a sidewalk along 64th Ave to run by gravel ponds. The trail ends at the batting cages at mile 3.8.

To reach the trail's continuation, follow 64th west to Federal Blvd, then turn left and head to the creek (5.0). The trail restarts on the northwest corner of Federal and the river. Quickly the trail leaves the industry and ducks under I-76 into the Lowell Ponds State Wildlife Area (trailhead on Lowell Blvd south of I-76). Enjoy the wide green belt, because houses soon squeeze the trail again. Soon it threads its way between quarries and the interstate, crossing under the highway twice and Sheridan once (6.9). This portion of the trail ends at 52nd (7.5), but signs direct you through a quiet neighborhood: Cross onto Gray St, follow that to the end, then jog right on Clear Creek Dr to the trail (7.7).

The trail now passes through quiet areas, some wooded. After passing under Wadsworth Blvd (8.9) into Johnson Park, it

enters its most idyllic stretch. No longer does it follow the freeway; instead the greenbelts and parks string together.

An unmarked junction at mile 10.6 presents an option: straight ahead the trail ends at the Kipling St trailhead (10.8). To continue the trail, cross the bridge onto side streets once more. From Independence Ct, turn right on 41st Ave and then follow the side trail as it winds under Kipling (11.1) and back to 41st. Take this street west to find the trail at the parking area (11.6).

This is the trail's wildest area. As you cross the bridge, listen to the creek gurgle and the birds sing. Soon the trees thin out as you reach Prospect Park (12.2), another trail access point with ball fields and restrooms. You then ride by several reclaimed gravel pits, now well-formed ponds. Another trailhead with picnic tables beckons before crossing under Youngfield St (13.3 miles).

The trail concludes with a long run between Coors property and a barren boulder-filled creek. The trail crosses the creek (13.9) then runs beside the busy highway CO58. At mile 14.5 trees provide a buffer, but by then it's nearly too late. The trail ends abruptly at 14.8 miles, just shy of the McIntyre St exit from the highway.

WHAT ELSE:

Clear Creek runs through Golden before entering the plains. This quaint town, home of Colorado School of Mines, generates a homey feel on the edge of the metro area. Known across the country as the home of

Coors beer, this town does offer attractions for the casual visitor as well as the out-of-town guest.

Top on the attractions lists, of course, would be the Coors Brewery Tour. Each year 350,000 people take advantage of the half-hour tour of the world's largest single brewing facility. From 13,000-gallon copper blending kettles to malting and bottling departments, you can see the Rocky Mountain spring water changed into one of America's favorite beverages. Of course, the tour ends in the tasting room, where of-age visitors can sample fresh beer on tap.

Another popular site lies on 44th Ave east of town. The Colorado Railroad Museum contains dozens of locomotives, cabooses, and other cars scattered around the twelve-acre grounds. On many you can climb aboard and pretend. Highlights include a train car made from parts of a Buick, Peirce Arrow, Ford truck, and a railroad engine; a scale model HO train running through a miniature mountain range; and the Big Boy, the largest style train engine ever built.

Lodging and restaurants are available in Golden. The city also hosts Self-Propulsion, one of the metro areas most noted bike shops.

TRAIL: *Highline Canal Trail*

Water, as it did throughout the state, figured prominently in Denver's history. With the seasonal flow of the Platte and its feeding creeks too unreliable to build a city around, early settlers had to find another solution. The obvious answer: irrigation.

Businessmen quickly generated plans to dam the river and marshal its waters, redirecting the flow to where it would do them the most good. Scores of canals and plans sprung up, but the most extensive by far was the Highline Canal.

From an outlet in Waterton Canyon, the canal traced a 74-mile route along a high-elevation line snaking across the plains. Construction, which begun in 1879, took four years and $650,000 to complete. It was designed to carry nearly three-quarters of a billion gallons of water per day, but actually averages only one-tenth of that -- 71 million gallons.

Today it is one of the area's most popular recreation paths. Over 800,000 people use it each year. The sometimes paved, sometimes dirt trail following it runs from Chatfield State Park to Environmental Park near Buckley Air Force Base. The southwestern portion does not connect directly with the sections further north; a three-quarter mile ride on Colorado Blvd is required to link the different halves.

TRAIL:	*Highline Canal Southwest / Arapahoe County*
DISTANCE:	*19.6 miles*
SURFACE:	*dirt/gravel*
DIFFICULTY:	*easy, but several street crossings*

The northern trailhead for this trail segment lies on Colorado Blvd south of Hampden Ave. The actual trail picks up on the south side of Hampden, where the canal leaves the Wellshire Municipal Golf Course. It passes well-kept (and often pricy) homes on large lots. After crossing Colorado Blvd (mile 1.0) (watch out for the traffic!) the trail circles Three Pond Park, the first of the open spaces it traverses. As you head further into Cherry Hills Village the homes grow even nicer, and the canal resembles a wild but narrow creek.

At 1.9 miles the trail crosses Quincy Ave, entering the 'remote' stretch of the trail. Quickly the surrounding mansions drop away, leaving rolling, wooded fields. Soon you curve to circle a wide open space with a lake, trees, and a spectacular mountain backdrop. This luscious open space remains even after passing under Belleview Ave (3.9) into Greenwood Village (be careful not to miss the ramp down on the right). Now houses crowd one side of the canal as it cuts a tight curve and heads west, then swings back southeast. The area turns more farm-like until it crosses Orchard Rd (6.7) and leaves Greenwood Village.

At mile 6.9 the Little Dry Creek Trail branches off this trail. To stay on Highline Canal, cross the creek and veer northwest past tightly packed (but still pricy) homes. Horse properties still dot the area. At 8.5 miles the trail crosses University Blvd (beware of the heavy traffic) and continues past landed properties.

Your arrival at Julia deKoevend Park marks the temporary end of solitude. As you pass Goodson Recreation Center (11.4), a good place to catch this trail, noise from University interrupts

134

the quiet; be careful of cars turning into the Rec Center parking. Follow the trail along the edge of the park, passing the connection to the Big Dry Creek Trail (11.5) as you again veer north.

The trail now winds through more middle-class neighborhoods. It passes Southwood Park (13.0) before turning commercial as it crosses (13.6) then parallels Broadway. To the west the trail looks down on schools and parks, giving you an unobstructed view of the peaks of the Front Range.

The trail re-crosses Broadway (14.2) to pass more houses and apartments, then crosses it a last time with the light at Ridge Rd. The trail soon cuts away from the businesses, heading south to wild Horseshoe Park. The Lee Gulch trail runs through the park, intersecting our path at mile 16.2.

The trail now winds through more residential neighborhoods, with numerous connections to the adjoining neighborhoods. The houses take on a richer tone, with mega-condos and ranchettes predominating. As the trail begins its final eastward turn, some magnificent vistas of the mountains open up.

At 18.3 miles the trail crosses Mineral Ave (no light) into aptly named Writer's Vista Park. To the southwest, mountains cut a jagged horizon over the blue waters of McLellan Reservoir. The trail stays north of the reservoir as it traverses an open space before crossing County Line Rd (19.3), finally merging with the Centennial trail (19.6).

TRAIL: *Highline Canal Central / Denver - Aurora*
DISTANCE: *13.8 miles*
SURFACE: *paved*
DIFFICULTY: *easy, but several street crossings*

Pick up this trail segment at Colorado Blvd and Hampden Ave. The trail uses the sidewalk on the east side of Colorado as it heads north to meet the canal emerging from the golf course. It turns east into Eisenhower Park, then follows the greenbelt between neighborhoods to cross under I-25 (mile 1.7). Side paths allow access to the neighborhoods.

The canal cuts lazy 'S' turns as it runs between houses east of the highway. A traffic lights eases your crossing of Holly St & Yale Ave (2.3), but you usually are not so lucky. You cross Holly again at mile 3.2, and cross Yale twice more (4.0, 5.4) at either end of James A. Bible Park. Be careful of the traffic at these and other crossings.

As the canal approaches Cherry Creek, the houses thin out a bit, revealing spectacular mountain vistas. Eventually horse properties appear after Quebec St (6.4). Soon you can see cyclists on the Cherry Creek Trail as the waterways parallel each other; they finally join at mile 8.0.

The trails quickly split again, and the canal heads north outside Los Verdes Country Club. North of Iliff Ave (9.2) the

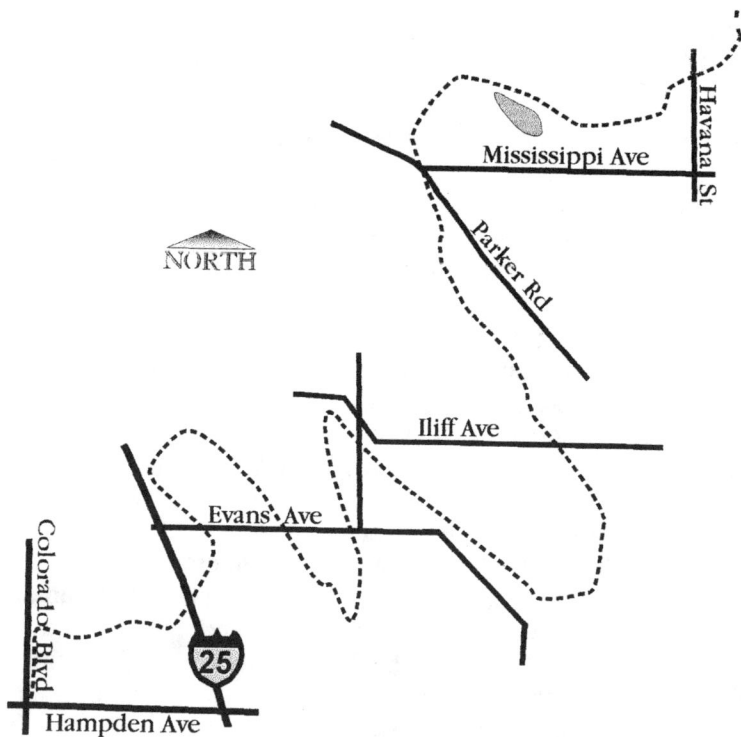

NORTH

neighborhoods turn upscale again, with large lots and horse properties a common sight. After crossing Florida Ave you pass an apartment area, then cross the Leetsdale/Mississippi/Parker Rd intersection to leave the crowded area behind.

For a change of pace, you now follow the trail through peaceful Fairmount Cemetery. After leaving the grounds at Valenta St (12.0), you pass by (and below) Windsor Lake before passing through one last neighborhood in Denver. The trail crosses Havana Ave (13.6) into Arapahoe County, and quickly reaches Expo Park (13.8) in Aurora. From here you can follow the trail further northeast, or you can head south on the Westerly Creek trail.

TRAIL:	*Highline Canal Northeast / Aurora*
DISTANCE:	*12.7 miles*
SURFACE:	*paved*
DIFFICULTY:	*easy, but several street crossings*

Pick up this segment on the west end of Expo Park (on Alameda Ave east of Havana St), where the Westerly Creek Trail meets the Highline Canal. Follow the edge of the park, and cross Alameda Ave (mile 0.5) into a nice neighborhood.

You now ride through 1960s-vintage subdivisions just south of Del Mark Park. The homes are well-kept, each with their own personality (unlike the cookie-cutter complexes so popular with builders today). After crossing Peoria St (1.8) just south of the park, the trail drops south to pass Lyn Knoll Elementary School (2.2) before heading due east. It forms the northern border of Aurora Hills Golf Course before entering an industrial area.

At I-225 the trail jogs north onto 2nd Ave to cross under the highway (3.2). Turn right on Abilene St, and the trail (and canal) pick up again on your left. The area is open and undeveloped until you cross Sable Blvd (3.6), where the houses begin again. You now bear southeast by more modern homes, passing Heritage Park and, beyond it, the courthouse.

Across Chambers Rd (4.1) lies Delaney Farm, a city-owned open space area filled with dirt fields and prairie dogs.. The trail dips south to Alameda Ave, where it intersects with the Tollgate Creek Trail (4.8). This trail runs south five miles through the heart of Aurora. Our trail continues on, quickly changing to a northern tack past condos, apartments, and (eventually) the Community College of Aurora (6.0). Be sure to check out the mountain vistas to the west.

The trail crosses 6th Ave at Chambers Rd, then curves away from the main street. The feel is more rural here, with horses in the fields and space between the different neighborhoods. It passes behind Hinkley High School (7.5) and comes upon a horse arena – a sure sign we're leaving the city behind. On the

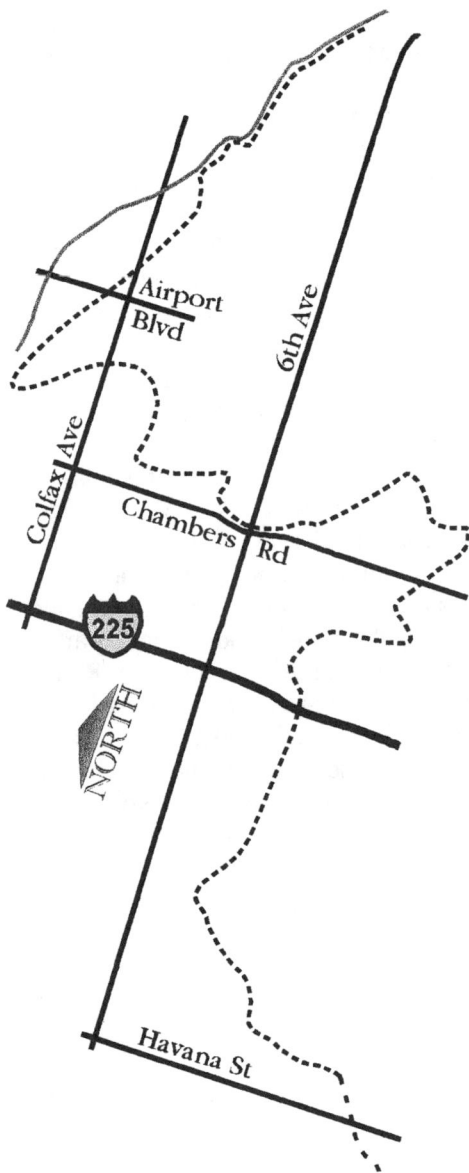

far side of Laredo St (8.2), a sign introduces man-made nesting boxes used to lure wildlife (such as kestrels, flickers, bats and wrens) back to the area. Stop to read about them, and you may learn something. (Did you know that bats will eat six hundred mosquitos an hour? I think I'll invite a few to my next barbecue.)

The canal crosses Colfax Ave (8.6) into the Norfolk Glen subdivision. At the trails northern extension, it curves around to present you with your first view of Sand Creek. A virtual forest along the waterway anchors a greenbelt nearly a mile wide. Work is proceeding on a trail that will eventually run the length of Sand Creek, from its intersection with this trail to the Platte River. This will provide an important link in the northern part of Denver's trail network.

Watch for horses on this stretch of the trail; they use this area frequently. Continue following the canal until you reach Airport Rd (10.1), where you have options. Those who like crossing heavy traffic can shoot across Airport to a small triangle of land above Friendly Village, then make an uncontrolled crossing of US40 (Colfax). An easier alternative is to follow the sidewalk to the Airport/Colfax intersection (10.2.4), then cross both roads with the lights. The trail continues at Colfax and 14th Dr, following 14th as it angles southeast through very rural terrain.

At mile 10.8 the trail passes between Springhill Municipal Golf Course and an RV storage lot. Soon Sand Creek reaches the trail with its complement of trees, and the Highline Canal breaks to the north. The trail continues east along the golf course, then dips south into Environmental Park. When it again turns east (11.4), you could almost picture yourself in Kansas or Nebraska: wild grasslands stretch to the trees filling the bottomland. The path rolls along, generally above the forested floodplain, as it winds through the mostly undeveloped park. (The view on the return leg is awesome, with the Front Range rising above the grassy plain – you can imagine how early settlers must have felt!) Toward the trail's end there is a picnic table, shelter, and a small parking lot (but with no road leading to it). It finally ends at mile 7.9, not at a road but at what looks like a rodeo facility.

TRAIL: *Platte River Greenway*

The Platte River Trail ranks as the longest continuous off-street trail in the metro area and, as of early 1999, in the state. The Highline Canal is much longer, of course, but interrupted in its middle by a stretch on Colorado Blvd. The routes in Summit County run longer, but include a mile of on-street in Frisco.

It's only fitting, then, that the Platte Trail also ranks as one of the first. For years the river existed as a wasteland, a magnet for urban debris. Its banks were strewn with discarded cement blocks, car tires and car bodies, and assorted trash – a virtual open sewer . The 1965 flood focused attention on the river, though, and started talk of rehabilitating the waterway. In 1974 Denver's mayor appointed a commission to save the river. It took years, but the Platte River Greenway is now the jewel of the urban trail system, and a shining example to other cities.

The centerpiece of the Greenway system is Confluence Park. Located where Cherry Creek flows into the Platte, it served as the birthplace of Denver. Now it lies in the center of the tourist district, adjacent to the city's biggest attractions.

To get to Confluence Park, get off I-25 at Speer Blvd and head east. Turn right on Elitch Cir and right on Little Raven St (the first street). You can park here, or turn left on 15th St and left on Platte St to the REI (formerly Forney Transportation Museum) and Ocean Journey/Children's Museum area.

WHAT ELSE:

The Greenway runs by several attractions. Near Confluence Park lies Ocean Journey and the Children's Museum, with the roller coasters of Elitch Gardens across the River. On the south end, South Platte Park and Chatfield State Park offer an escape from the urban mass.

TRAIL: *Platte River North / Denver - Adams County*
DISTANCE: *11.7 miles*
SURFACE: *paved*
DIFFICULTY: *easy*

From Confluence Park and Cherry Creek, head north carefully through the plaza (it may be easier to walk bikes through here). Follow the twisting, downhill walkway past the rapids and follow the signs to pass under 15th St. At 0.4 miles cross the river on an old railroad bridge and drop back into the river bed. This stretch of the river is filled with parks reclaimed from various supply yards and landfills.

After passing under 38th St (2.4), the trail enters Globeville Park. It climbs through the park to a small picnic pavilion before dropping down and crossing over the river. (From Globeville, you can take Arkins Ct to McFarland Dr to reach the Denver Coliseum, less than a half mile away.) On the west bank a newly paved section of the trail speeds you north to Franklin St (3.8), where you again cross the river. The trail starts anew on the corner of Race St, heading into Adams County.

As you pass Riverside Cemetery, the trail crosses a diversion canal into a wild strip. Watch for native critters here – you may get lucky and spy a beaver. The trail again crosses to the west bank (5.3), where it will remain. As we head north, the river regains some of its historical character as a lazy, meandering stream. The only reminders left of the city are the utility towers and power lines that tower above.

I-270 and its traffic passes overhead at mile 6.2, leaving no nearby roads. After dipping under I-76, pay attention to your choices: The bridge to the right goes over the Platte, but quickly peters out. Straight ahead the path simply goes down to the river. The correct choice is the bridge to the left, taking you over Clear Creek. On the far bank (7.2) the Clear Creek Trail heads west; the Platte trail continues to the right.

From I-76 on, picnic tables and park benches dot the trail,

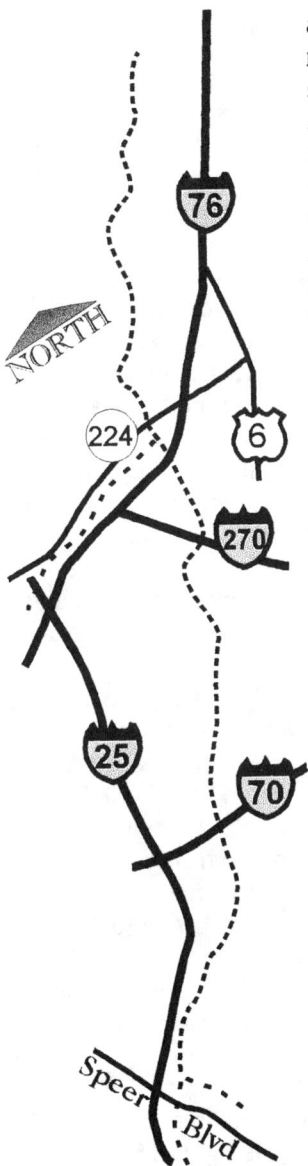

as do small parks wherever roads meet the river. Wetlands and ponds soon flank the river as it continues to snake downstream. After passing 78th Ave/Steele St (8.0), you are alone in the 'wilderness' until Colorado Blvd (9.2). The trail then heads into its last miles. Ponds and lakes on both sides lend an out-of-town feel. Behind you the mountains form a beautiful backdrop for the scene. After two miles of solitude, the trail finally ends at McKay Rd (11.7).

TRAIL: *Platte River South / Denver - Sheridan - Littleton*
DISTANCE: *16.0 miles*
SURFACE: *paved*
DIFFICULTY: *easy*

From Confluence Park, head south along the river's west bank. In spring or summer months, you may see inner-tubers or kayakers playing in the river. On the opposite shore the roller coasters of Elitch Gardens rise against a backdrop of skyscrapers; and you can hear the screams as Twister II roars down the track. To your right Ocean Journey, Denver's new aquarium, rises from the land, followed by Children's Museum.

At 0.9 miles a bike bridge leads across the river to connect with a path along the east shore, but our trail proceeds straight ahead. With Elitch's now behind you, the scenery turns more to parking lots and grimy buildings. Lakewood Gulch Trail branches inland at 1.2 miles, while we continue hugging the river. A bridge near 8th Ave takes us over the river (2.0), landing in Frog Hollow, a narrow park squeezed between the Platte and I-25.

The interstate soon hugs the river closely, forcing the trail to cross back to the west bank (3.1). The trail jogs away from the river to circle small Johnson-Habitat Park, but veers back on the far side. A trail spur crosses Platte River Dr into Vanderbilt Park (4.3) just before the trail crosses under Santa Fe Dr, with traffic now hemming in the river (and the trail) on both sides.

The trail leaves the traffic after crossing the river into Overland Lake Park (5.3). Continue under Florida Ave (5.5), which provides the connection to the Sanderson Gulch Trail, and Evans Ave (6.2) through more residential scenery. On the far side of Evans the trail enters Frontier Park, crosses the river and jumps into another stretch of industrial scenery.

The trail finally leaves the road at 8.4 as an expansive view of the Front Range mountains opens up ahead. In another short distance the Bear Creek Trail branches to the right (8.6), while

the Greenway continues beside the Englewood Municipal Golf Course. South of the golf course, the trail enters its grimiest territory, with gravel bars in the river and junk businesses (crushed cars and crumbling concrete) lining the banks.

It doesn't last, and soon you're wheeling along beside Centennial Golf & Tennis Club. At mile 11.6 you hit a junction; both branches cross under Bowles Ave and merge again south of the road (12.2). By now trees again shade the river, and you leave development behind. The side entrance to Hudson Gardens beckons at mile 12.4, and is worth a visit. The Lee Gulch Trail splits off at 12.9 miles, while the main trail continues into South Platte Park (13.4).

The remaining length of the trail runs through the park, which protects the river as it leaves Chatfield State Park. Wetlands and ponds (reclaimed gravel pits) line the trail, and interpretive signs describe the area and wildlife. The peaceful atmosphere surrounds you until you cross under C470 (15.8), and the trail ends at the Centennial Trail junction (16.0).

INDEX

Excerpt from
UNDERWEAR BY THE ROADSIDE

Sue hit the sack early, while I stayed up to read. At 9:30 I put down the book, turned off the flashlight, and relaxed to the murmur of the White River. As I collected the energy to move to the tent and my waiting sleeping bag, I realized I had company. In the half-light of the star-lit night, I could see he was well dressed, wearing pressed pants and a print shirt. He was near forty, and looked deep in thought, neither smiling nor frowning. "Didn't mean to startle you," he said. "Just out for my evening stroll."

He sat at the picnic table with me and began to talk. I listened, too tired to contribute much, but interested in hearing of his Amish life.

"I don't always get along with my neighbors here," he confided. "Sometimes they don't care for how we do things. For example, on an Amish farm, we always leave a field wild for the birds and insects to have a place to feed. If I tried that in town, they'd have a fit. Call it an eyesore and probably fine me.

"Nature has a way of taking care of things, if we'd let it. If you have an infestation of insects one year, you'll probably get more birds to balance them out. Used to be, when you had too much tall grass, you'd have extra bison to eat it."

He rambled on, his voice sometimes flowing softly like the river just out of sight, other times turning strident. "People shouldn't have more kids than they can support. The Amish, we take care of our own. We run benefits for widows and orphans, because they're part of our lives. Me, I had a son at age fourteen, and I had to take care of him and his mother. I did, too, for eighteen years."

He paused, and I turned to see him with his eyes closed, his face lined with sadness. "When my son left to go

149

among the English – that's what we call anyone not an Amish, Mennonite, or Quaker, the 'English' – I warned him he'd lose his way, he wouldn't make it. After four years out there, he took poison and killed himself." His voice grew softer. "He kept saying, 'I can't find the answers.' I tried to tell him, "There aren't any answers to find because there are no questions.' By twenty-one or twenty-two, you should know the path you are on in life. If you stray from that path, you're going to get confused, and look for ever more answers to which there are no questions."

He lapsed into silence, the white noise of the flowing river surrounding us. When he spoke again, his voice had regained its strength. "The trouble is, people always need a thrill, they always need to fell good. They don't realize life isn't all 'feel good,' there's pain involved, and 'feel good' is relative. If I have a bad toothache, I feel good when the ache is cured."

After nearly an hour he left, vanishing into the night much as he had appeared, leaving behind not only a name. Subdued but fascinated, I joined Sue in our nylon castle, drifting off with his words replaying in my head.

About the Author

Glen Hanket was raised in Boulder, CO – but please don't hold that against him. A software engineer by trade, he writes books and gives speeches on bicycling, walking, and the evils of litter in his 'spare' time. An inveterate traveler, he has a dream of visiting all the country's National Park sites.

Looking for the ultimate in trashy reading?
Need an in-depth guide to Denver's trails?
Our books are available at finer bookstores and sports
stores, or you can order direct from:

CAK Publishing
PO Box 953
Broomfield, CO   80038

Please send me _____ copies of *Underwear by the Roadside*
Please send me _____ copies of *Take A Bike!*
I am enclosing $12.95 per book (less 10% for orders of
two or more books), plus shipping and handling of
$1.50 per book. Colorado residents, please add $0.39 tax
for one book or $.30 each for two or more books.
Send check or money order (no CODs) to the above
address. Please allow up to three weeks for shipping.

SHIP TO:

Name: _____

Address: _____

City/State: _____ *ZIP:* _____